Business Owner's Guide To

Accounting & Bookkeeping

By José Placencia, Bruce Welge, and Don Oliver

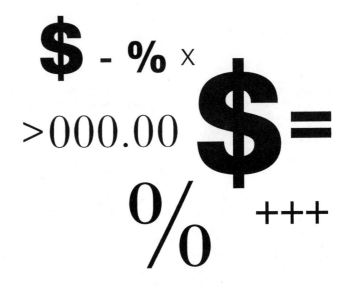

Edited by Constance C. Dickinson

The Oasis Press® / PSI Research
Grants Pass, Oregon

Published by The Oasis Press®
© 1991, 1997 by José Placencia, Bruce Welge, and Don Oliver

This publication is designed to provide accurate and authoritative information in regard to the subject matter covered. It is sold with the understanding that the publisher is not engaged in rendering legal, accounting, or other professional service. If legal advice or other expert assistance is required, the services of a competent professional person should be sought.

> *— from a declaration of principles jointly adopted by a committee of the American Bar Association and a committee of publishers.*

Book Designer and Editor: Constance C. Dickinson
Typographer: Jan Olsson

Please direct any comments, questions, or suggestions regarding this book to The Oasis Press®/PSI Research:

Editorial Department
P.O. Box 3727
Central Point, OR 97502
(541) 479-9464
FAX (541) 476-1479
info@psi-research.com *(email)*

The Oasis Press® is a Registered Trademark of Publishing Services, Inc., an Oregon corporation doing business as PSI Research.

Library of Congress Cataloging-in-Publication Data

Placencia, José F.
    Business owner's guide to accounting & bookkeeping / José Placencia, Bruce Welge, and Don Oliver. — 2nd ed.
        p.   cm. — (PSI successful business library)
    Includes index.
    ISBN 1-55571-381-5 (pbk.)
    1. Small business—Accounting.   I. Welge, Bruce, 1946–
II. Oliver, Don, 1954–   III. Title.   IV. Series.
HF5657.P58   1997
657'.9042—dc21   97-37067

Printed in the United States of America
Second Edition 10 9 8 7 6 5 4

 Printed on recycled paper when available.

Tables of Contents

Chapter 3 *Understanding Financial Statements*

Chapter 4 *Be Your Own Bookkeeper*

Chapter 4 (continued)

Chapter 5 *Automated Bookkeeping*

Appendix I *The Accounting Cycle*

Appendix II *Financial Analysis Tools*

Glossary *Accounting Terms*

Illustrations

Figure

Tables and Exhibits

Chapter 2

Chapter 3

Chapter 4

Chapter 4 (continued)

Chapter 5

Appendix I

Appendix II

Chapter 1

The Basics for Success

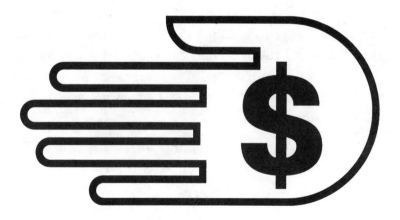

What Is My Need to Know?

A question often posed by many business owners and managers is "Why should I concern myself with bookkeeping and finance?" It is unfortunate that this question is most often asked by business owners who are doomed to see their business fail. The level of ignorance of accounting in the general business population is astoundingly high. In fact, the level of interest in learning accounting ranks only above that of learning ancient Greek or Latin. But beware: 95% of all new businesses fail within the first five years of operation.

Independent statistical sources such as Dun & Bradstreet, which collect data on business failures, attribute these failures to various causes including inadequate working capital, management error, and catastrophic events. Yet, it is arguable that all business failures relate to a lack of understanding by the owner or manager of the basic economics of that business. Accounting and its related discipline, financial analysis, offer the business owner or manager the ability to comprehend the basic, underlying economics of a business.

Financial Statements

Many business owners feel that financial statements are a necessary evil imposed by the Internal Revenue Service, and are required only once a year on March 15 (the federal income tax filing deadline for businesses that end their accounting year on December 31). With this attitude, business owners often miss the opportunity to manage their business using reliable, up-to-date financial information. Such information can be obtained through the application of a well-designed and well-implemented accounting system that provides accurate and timely information.

When employed on a regular basis this accounting information can indicate problems, such as whether:

- Inventories are too high;
- Accounts receivable collections are taking too long;
- Machinery is becoming antiquated;
- The company would qualify for a loan (and for how much);
- Pricing is too low;
- Materials and inventory costs are too high; or
- The business is suffering from theft or labor inefficiency.

All of the above indications and information are available to you if you implement a functional accounting system. Learn how to use it and learn how to understand the financial statements and reports the system produces.

Accounting portrays in numerical terms the status of the business. Therefore, you need to place yourself in the position of being able to understand and translate, just as you would with the French language if you visited France.

One objective of this book is to introduce you, as a business owner or manager, to the concepts of basic financial information. This introduction to the language of accounting includes answers to several often-asked questions.

- What are the basic financial statements?
- What are their component parts?
- How do I analyze these financial statements?
- What is the basic accounting cycle?
- Can I perform the accounting functions myself?
- What are accounting systems, both manual and automated?
- How can I control my accounting system?

These are all very important questions, and the answers are important to you as a business owner or manager.

A number of financial statements are used by various companies for different purposes, they include:

- Statement of changes in owner's equity,
- Statement of changes in financial position,
- Funds flow statement, and
- Cash flow statement.

In addition, there are many others of more limited or specific application. However, two financial statements are universal in use and application — the balance sheet and the income statement (also called the profit and loss statement, statement of operations, or statement of income).

The balance sheet and income statement are used when business income tax returns are filed, when you apply for a loan, when you attempt to get bonding, when you attempt to sell your business to an outside party, when you try to raise capital from prospective partners or investors, and when you provide information to your suppliers or credit bureaus. The most important use of these statements, however, is in assessing the performance of your business.

The balance sheet and income statement provide a considerable amount of information regarding the operations and affairs of a business. Understanding this information is an important early step toward improving the results of your business.

Chapter 2, What Is a Financial Statement? illustrates these two basic financial statements. Formats for balance sheets and income statements are shown and the component parts of each financial statement is explained. There is nothing particularly difficult about these financial statements, once you overcome the initial feeling of being overwhelmed by them. It is important that every business owner and manager be able to read and understand the information presented in the financial statements.

Most business owners either do not have the knowledge or choose not to perform their own accounting function. The primary value of most business owners to their business lies in their sales or product knowledge and any time diverted from these functions can be detrimental to the growth and success of the business. Nevertheless, in many cases a business owner has the time to personally perform the accounting function but is afraid to do so because of lack of knowledge or lack of inclination.

If you decide to perform the accounting function yourself, you obviously need to understand the accounting cycle. Even though you may not be inclined to perform the accounting function yourself, it is essential for you to understand how the numbers in your business' financial statements were derived. For this you need a reasonable understanding of the sources of data and the concepts used in processing and presenting such data in your business' financial statements.

Even if you hire an outside party to perform your accounting function, you, as the owner of the business, should exercise certain controls over the function and review the data produced. Remember, the only picture of your business presented to much of the outside world is that created by your financial statements.

Outsiders' perception of your business is often based solely upon your financial statements.

What if you are paying taxes on income you did not earn? What if you cannot obtain bank credit, or supplier credit? What if you cannot obtain a fair price for your business when you try to sell it? These possibilities could be the result of inaccurate or misleading financial statements. It is your responsibility to know if your financial statements are wrong!

Chapter 2 will help you gain the necessary understanding to know when there is something wrong with your financial statements.

Techniques for Analysis

Chapter 3, Understanding Financial Statements, introduces various analytical techniques which are routinely applied in understanding financial statements. These are all measures used in evaluating a business' performance.

Many static and dynamic analytical tools are available, and this section introduces several basic techniques for evaluating the performance of your business. There are both internal and external benefits to your business derived from performing financial analysis. The external uses are largely beyond the control of the business owner or manager, and tend to be conducted by banks, loan companies, bonding companies, your suppliers, and potential purchasers of your business. Every one of these entities will perform evaluations introduced here.

By understanding how to perform these analyses yourself, you will be in a position to understand how the outside business world analyzes and perceives your business. You will thus be armed with the same techniques to analyze your business' performance, giving you a solid base upon which to make management decisions.

If you understand what a good business profile looks like, you can adjust the tactics, strategies, goals, and management of your business to achieve a more favorable profile. To that end, the external uses of financial analyses can be important to you as a business owner. Armed with this knowledge, you can manage your business affairs to improve your debt-to-equity ratio and qualify for a loan for which you may not have qualified before. You can work to improve your business' current or quick ratios, become a more attractive customer to your suppliers, and, perhaps, obtain credit or more favorable trade terms. You can position your business for sale, or manage the business so that the financial statements are more favorable for tax or inheritance purposes. By knowing where you have been and where you are now, it is much easier to see in which direction you should go. In business parlance, you are able to manage your business effectively.

Several types of analyses are introduced in Chapter 3. Ratio analysis, comparative analysis, and percentage-of-sales analysis are standard, easy-to-understand analytic tools used by external sources to evaluate your business' performance. These analytic tools take the balance sheet and the income statement and compare specific transaction accounts. Once you get used to the terminology, these analytic tools boil down to being simple arithmetic formulae applied to determine relationships between accounts. This is ratio analysis, and the resulting comparative numbers (or ratios) provide information on many aspects of your business including:

- What its liquidity is;
- What its debt coverage ability is;
- What its capacity for new debt is;
- How well it is collecting its receivables; and
- How suitable its inventory levels are.

Comparative analysis can take two forms. First, these techniques can be used to compare your business' performance against that of other companies in the same type of business. Second, they can be used to compare your business' performance for the current period against its performance in prior periods. This latter approach will enable you to identify trends that are occurring in your business.

Percentage-of-sales analysis looks at the different components of the income statement and permits you to assess the productivity of your business operations. This is the simplest evaluation method but one which, once understood, provides critical information both about your business and how it compares with industry averages.

The concepts and methods of budgeting and planning are also introduced. These techniques employ analysis and put the results into a format you can use to plan the future of your business. They also give you a benchmark for comparing predicted and actual performance. Besides helping you control your business, the budgeting and planning processes help you manage the way all successful small business owners do, by helping you understand the economics of the business.

The Accounting Cycle

In Chapter 4, Be Your Own Bookkeeper, the entire accounting cycle is explained, from source documentation to preparation of financial statements. It is not the intent of this section to turn an accounting novice into a bona fide accountant. It does, however, provide sufficient information to allow you to perform your own accounting function and understand where you may need specific assistance from a qualified accountant.

This chapter introduces three concepts of accounting. These are the concepts of double entry, debits and credits, and transaction accounts.

The tried-and-true law of physics, which decries that "for every action there is an equal and opposite reaction," correlates well to the accounting function for understanding the double-entry system. That is, every event (transaction) in the day-to-day operation of a business is recorded twice — once as a "positive" action, and once (in an equal amount) as a "negative" reaction.

Double-entry accounting affects accounts in either a "positive" or "negative" manner, depending upon the nature of the account, and whether the transaction will increase or decrease that account. By using debits and credits, the transaction and its effect on the corresponding accounts can be clearly seen.

This chapter clearly defines debits and credits, and provides a number of transaction examples to guide you through the theory and practice of using debits and credits in your accounting function.

In order to simplify the process of recording day-to-day business events, transactions are often given short descriptive names which describe the type of transaction (accounts receivable, rent expense, accounts payable). Rather than recording the transaction as "paying the landlord the monthly rent," a more concise description is simply "rent expense," since it is an expense (cost of doing business) and exclusively involves the act of paying rent. These are known as transaction accounts.

The next chapter looks at original entries. Original entries can come from both paper (checks, invoices) and nonpaper (bank charges, payroll-related expenses) sources. Paper sources are important for supporting information on financial statements — in the event of a tax audit, for example — while nonpaper sources (generally recurring transactions) require some internal means of recording, such as a schedule.

Chapter 4 also examines journals and ledgers, where each transaction is recorded. A business might use a combination of journals, including the cash disbursements journal, the cash receipts journal, and the general journal. All journals, however, fall into one of two categories: two-column or multicolumn. The two-column journal is most frequently seen as the general journal, with the columns noting whether the transaction was a debit or a credit to the particular account.

The multicolumn journal has one debit or credit column; if there is one debit column, the remainder of the columns should be credit columns, and vice versa. In the example, Exhibit L-2, Cash Disbursements Journal, there is one credit column (cash), since each transaction involves a negative (credit) influence on the cash of the business. The remainder of the columns are debit columns, since each transaction will have a debit effect on the various expense accounts (merchandise expense, advertising expense, utility expense, or other expense).

Once all transactions for a given accounting period have been entered into the appropriate journals, the next step is to transfer (post) all entries from the journals to the general ledger. The general ledger is a group of two-column pages, one page for each transaction account. The general ledger serves a dual purpose: it groups together all transactions within a given accounting period for each particular transaction account, thus facilitating an analysis of each account. Since all transaction accounts are totaled, it also simplifies the preparation of financial statements.

Finally, Chapter 4 illustrates how financial statements are prepared through the medium of a working trial balance. In a working trial balance, the individual accounts are listed and allocated to either the balance sheet or the income statement. When completed, the balances shown on the working trial balance are the final balances that are included in the financial statements. Then, the final step is to transfer these balances into your chosen balance sheet and income statement formats.

Accounting Systems

Whether you are operating a manual or computerized accounting function, your business has an accounting system. Many time-saving systems are available which can simplify the accounting function.

For manual systems, there are a number of one-write bookkeeping systems available through business stationers or mail order suppliers. These systems allow the accountant to perform multiple tasks simultaneously, reducing the duplication of paperwork and saving time. Many of the work functions that are tedious to maintain, or are not properly maintained, can be covered using these one-write systems.

Chapter 5, Automated Bookkeeping, introduces the concept of these systems and gives a general description of their use.

The chapter also discusses computer hardware and software. In addition to hints on what to look for in a computerized system, we have indicated some controls which, if applied, should ensure that your automated system provides useful information. It is important to note, however, that many of these controls are of the common-sense variety and apply equally well to both manual and computerized accounting systems.

An important concept in management is that the most usable information should be produced with the least effort. From a systems perspective, this means that your accounting system should be designed so that it produces meaningful information on a timely basis with a minimum amount of input and clerical effort.

Extremely detailed information may be impressive, but unless you use it there was no point in producing it. Therefore, your system should produce little more than what you will use in making your business decisions. It is usually more important to obtain summary information quickly than it is to receive detailed information many months later. You, as the business owner or manager, must understand your accounting system and ensure that it produces information which is important to you.

After reading this book, you will have a feel for the value of financial statements and analytic tools. These, combined with good accounting information upon which to apply these tools, are the cornerstones of your business decisions. Remember, most businesses fail because of a lack of understanding of their economics. Becoming familiar (and comfortable) with your financial reports and financial statements is a major step toward helping you understand the economics and realities of your business.

Finally, even if you are not interested in performing your own accounting function but make the effort to understand it, you will have improved your edge over your competitors through a sound knowledge of your own business.

Where the numbers come from is very important — only double-entry bookkeeping prevents the books from being out of balance. If garbage is posted to your books, the financial statements produced will be garbage. Your system will not tell you this unless you understand the process and ensure adequate controls are in place. Just as a business that is inept in sales and marketing will fail and a business that cannot manufacture well will fail, so too, will a business that lacks financial competence fail.

Your accounting system is a tool to be used to understand and control your business operations. The better you understand it and ensure that it gives you the financial information you need, the better you are placed to manage your business. From this you gain the extra potential to build a more successful and more profitable business.

Chapter 2

What Is a Financial Statement?

The Importance of Understanding

Many small business owners believe that the usefulness of financial statements begins and ends with business tax returns. This misconception is understandable, since most small business owners may be skilled at sales, service, or manufacturing, but unskilled in bookkeeping. Nevertheless, it is regrettable; a basic understanding of financial statements could save some failing businesses and help some subsistent businesses to thrive.

Many people have heard the story of the business owner who was losing money on each unit of product sold and attempted to make up the loss with increased volume. Fewer have heard of the owner whose year-end financial statements showed that the business had made a taxable profit, but there was insufficient cash in the bank to pay the tax obligation. Such stories are humorous, unless they happen to you.

The sad reality is that these situations occur very often, and they are often avoidable. The business owner who wanted to make up a loss with increased volume may be suffering from labor inefficiency, overly expensive material costs, inflated overhead, waste, theft, or inadequate pricing. An increase in volume may only increase the business' losses. The profitable business with no cash to pay taxes may be growing too fast and may have over invested in machinery, fixtures, accounts receivable, inventory, or some combination of assets.

The best way to analyze the possible problems of the above companies is to understand financial statements. A properly conceptualized and adequately maintained accounting system will provide the basis for comprehending the fundamental economics of any business' activity, from ABC Pet Supply Company to General Motors. Financial statements — the balance sheet and the income statement — are primary sources of information concerning the operation of a business. In the hands of a knowledgeable business owner they are of inestimable value.

There is a historical adage: "Those who do not understand the lessons of history are doomed to repeat it." There should be an economic counterpoint: "Those who do not understand the economics of their business are doomed to fail."

Never lose sight of the fact that business is an economic activity. As such, it has a cost structure and associated revenue potential. A business owner has the personal obligation to understand the basic economics of the business and to monitor the company's performance over time. Performance monitoring can only be accomplished by the generation of accurate, relevant financial information and by an accurate interpretation of the financial statements.

The balance sheet provides a static "snapshot" of a business. It lists and valuates everything the business owns and what it owes, and shows the aggregate earnings or losses of the business from inception. It provides this information for only one moment in time, the close of business on the last day of the reporting period — usually the end of a month, quarter, or year. A proper balance sheet will usually indicate the period involved in the document heading — for example, "Dated as of December 31, 19xx." It is the essential nature of a balance sheet to provide information reflective of business on one particular day.

The income statement provides dynamic information for a business. It lists and valuates all of the product (or service) sales, and all of the expenses incurred by a business in all of its production, sales, and administrative activities. The income statement provides this information for a specific period of time, either for one month, quarter, or year. A proper income statement heading will usually read, "For the period ending December 31, 19xx."

The concepts of the balance sheet and income statement are easily understood. Perhaps it is this relative ease that causes too many business owners to virtually ignore financial statements. The accounting function is all too often considered "the other side of the tracks" in business organizations, including many Fortune 1,000 companies. Financial statements are frequently under utilized, often at great cost to the company.

Every business owner knows that a balance sheet and income statement must be provided annually to the Internal Revenue Service, state income tax authorities, and some municipal income tax authorities. In terms of value to a business owner, this is the least valuable use of financial statements. Five general uses for such statements are as follows:

- Analysis
- Credit
- Business relationships
- Valuation
- Reporting

There are numerous reasons for preparing and understanding timely financial statements. The balance sheet and income statement are integral parts of running a business, and understanding them is a critical responsibility of the business owner.

The Balance Sheet

The balance sheet is a financial statement which presents summary information of a business' assets, liabilities, and net worth. These essential facts can be used by a business owner to assist in managing a company, and by outside entities to evaluate creditworthiness, various tax obligations, or to evaluate the company.

The following information discusses each important section and presents examples of balance sheets. The data is designed to present essential facts about the balance sheet, and ultimately to facilitate a business owner's management process.

The balance sheet is essential in order to accomplish these basic business functions:

- Presenting the financial status at the end of each current period (month, quarter, or year);
- Spotting changes which have occurred within the business (by comparing current and previous balance sheets); and
- Managerial control, as a basis for establishing goals and budgets to improve the company's performance.

The function of a balance sheet is to illustrate the financial well-being, or lack thereof, of a business. The statement is segregated into three sections: assets, liabilities, and equity.

Assets

A list, with current values, of everything the business owns, including cash, receivables, fixed assets, and intangible assets. See Table 1.

Table 1 – List of Typical Assets

Asset	Includes
Cash	Petty cash
	Cash in bank
	Cash investments
	Accounts receivable
	Prepaid expenses (i.e. business insurance)
Inventory	Merchandise
	Raw materials
	Work-in-process
	Finished goods
Fixed Assets	Land
	Buildings
	Leasehold improvements
	Machinery
	Office equipment
	Depreciation
Other Assets	Goodwill
	Deposits

Liabilities

A list of everything the business owes and to whom, including suppliers, employees, banks, and tax authorities.

Table 2 – List of Typical Liabilities

Liability	Includes
Short-term Payables (obligations due in less than one year)	Accounts payable
	Accrued payable (including a portion of long-term payables)
	Taxes payable
	Wages payable
	Short-term notes payable
Long-term Payables (obligations due in more than one year)	Mortgage payable
	Bank loan payable
	Notes payable
	Deferred taxes payable

Equity

A list, with current values, of all of the business' capital stock issuances, and its aggregate profit or loss since inception.

Table 3 – List of Typical Equity

Equity	Includes
Capital Stock	Common stock
	Paid in surplus
	Preferred stock
	Treasury stock
Retained Earnings	Current year profit or loss
	Cumulative profit or loss from prior years

The equity of a business will equal the difference between its assets and liabilities — what it owns minus what it owes. The primary formula for the balance sheet is the following:

Assets = Liabilities + Equity

Another form of the formula is as follows:

Equity = Assets − Liabilities

This difference, equity, also known as net worth, is a principal fact used by outside entities such as suppliers or banks to evaluate the financial health of a business.

The asset and liability sections of a balance sheet are segregated into current and long-term accounts. These designations define assets and liabilities that will: expire or be used up within one year (current); or exist for a period of more than one year (long-term).

The one-year criterion is useful for analysis. In current period evaluation, one might ask, "What is the present financial status of the business?" In long-term evaluation the question might be, "What will be the financial status in the future?"

Exhibit A illustrates the balance sheet in its entirety. There are various alternative formats; however, the essential components are shown here.

Exhibit A – Sample Balance Sheet

NuCorp, Inc.
Balance Sheet
As of December 31, 1995

Assets

Current Assets:

Cash in Bank	$ 30,000	
Accounts Receivable	150,000	
Employees' Advances	10,000	
Inventory	100,000	
Prepaid Expenses	20,000	
Total Current Assets		$310,000

Fixed Assets:

Land & Building	200,000	
Office Equipment	20,000	
Machinery & Equipment	150,000	
Leasehold Improvements	30,000	
Accumulated Depreciation	(50,000)	
Total Fixed Assets		350,000

Other Assets:

Deposits	10,000	
Goodwill	50,000	
Total Other Assets		60,000
Total Assets		$720,000

Exhibit A – Sample Balance Sheet (continued)

Liabilities

Current Liabilities:

Accounts Payable	$100,000	
Payroll Taxes Payable	25,000	
Interest Payable	15,000	
Wages Payable	10,000	
Current Portion – Long-term Note Payable	40,000	
Total Current Liabilities		$190,000

Long-term Liabilities:

Mortgage Payable	150,000	
Bank Loan Payable	100,000	
Total Long-term Liabilities		250,000
Total Liabilities		440,000

Shareholders' Equity:

Common Stock	100,000	
Retained Earnings – Current	60,000	
Retained Earnings – Prior	120,000	
Total Shareholders' Equity		280,000
Total Liabilities & Equity		$720,000

The balance sheet is a compilation of everything the company owns and owes. There is no detail of specific assets or liabilities. In this sample balance sheet the company is owed $150,000 by customers, and owes $100,000 to its suppliers. The balance sheet does not identify these individuals or companies; this kind of information should be maintained by the company in individual subsidiary lists such as accounts receivable and accounts payable ledgers.

The balance sheet is in balance according to the primary accounting formula: assets equal liabilities plus equity. In the sample balance sheet, assets equal $720,000, and liabilities ($440,000) plus equity ($280,000) also equal $720,000.

The Income Statement

The income statement, also known as a profit and loss statement or statement of income, is a financial statement which presents information on the operations of the company; specifically, whether the company made or lost money for the reporting period.

Whereas the balance sheet presents cumulative information on the company, the income statement presents the most current information. It is the easier statement to understand — either the company made money, or it lost money. The income statement is the basis for determining income tax obligations, levels of supportable debt by banks, and the owner's evaluation of the success of the business.

Earnings are the basis for valuation of a successful company. Stock markets value companies on the basis of "price:earnings" by multiplying the earnings per share by a multiple — a number usually between 5 and 20 — that is determined by future growth prospects. Whether the company made a profit or not is the ultimate score keeping function in business.

The following discusses the components of the income statement and various possible presentation formats. There is some variety in the format of income statements, depending upon the nature of the business.

The income statement is important in accomplishing the following processes:

- Determining the profitability of a company for a given period (month, quarter, or year);
- Providing comparative information on current period versus prior period economic activity; and
- Providing expense data relating to operating efficiency of the company.

Determining Profitability

The function of the income statement is to determine the profitability, or lack thereof, of a company. The statement can be divided into four sections:

Sales

The cumulative value of products or services sold by the company to its customers or clients.

Cost of sales

The product or service costs directly related to the production or merchandise cost of the items sold, including direct labor, materials, and overhead.

Expenses

The costs of all other business activity not related to the production or merchandise cost of the items sold, including Sales and Marketing, General and Administrative, and Research and Development.

Extraordinary

All other costs or revenues not related to the primary business activity of the company, including sales of company equipment, building, or land — for other than real estate companies. Extraordinary items do not normally occur in a small business.

Exhibits B and C, on the following pages, represent two formats for reporting the operating results of the same company. The numbers are exactly the same — in each case, the company sold $1.2 million worth of products and generated an after-tax profit of $60,000.

Deciding which format to use depends on who is going to examine the income statement. Exhibit C reveals far more information concerning the company than does Exhibit B. Therefore, the format in Exhibit C should be used for internal purposes and the format in Exhibit B should generally be used for external purposes.

Exhibit B – Basic Income Statement: Example 1

NuCorp, Inc.
Statement of Income
Period Ending December 31, 1995

Sales	$1,200,000
Cost of Sales	800,000
Gross Profit	400,000
Other Expenses:	
Marketing & Sales	140,000
General, Administrative	100,000
Research & Development	40,000
Total Other Expenses	280,000
Pre-tax Profit	120,000
Provision for Taxes	60,000
Net Income	$ 60,000

This income statement format is not appropriate for filing income tax returns. It is the basic format used by publicly held companies or smaller businesses providing profitability information to outside entities such as banks and creditors.

It is incumbent upon business owners and managers to know as much as possible about their business. Appropriate data and consistent accounting procedures provide an independent appraisal of business operations.

Exhibit C is the basic income statement format business owners should use for their own information. This statement contains proprietary information and, with the exception of tax authorities, you are under no obligation to share it with vendors, suppliers, or bankers. Use the format of Exhibit C for yourself and Exhibit B for outsiders.

Exhibit C – Basic Income Statement: Example 2

NuCorp, Inc.
Statement of Income
Period Ending December 31, 1995

Sales	$1,200,000
Cost of Sales	800,000
Gross Profit	400,000
Other Operating Expenses:	
Administrative Salaries	40,000
Rent Expense	12,000
Interest Expense	18,000
Legal & Accounting Expense	15,000
Office Supplies	5,000
Depreciation – Office Equipment	4,000
Janitorial Expense	3,000
Taxes & Licenses	2,000
Miscellaneous Administrative	1,000
Subcontract Labor – New Products	25,000
Research Materials	15,000
Sales Commissions	60,000
Advertising	30,000
Sales Promotion	15,000
Travel	8,000
Sales Brochures	7,000
Sales Salaries	20,000
Total Other Expenses	280,000
Pre-tax Profits	120,000
Provision for Taxes	60,000
Net Income	$ 60,000

The balance of this section will display more income statement formats. These additional formats are important because they convey more information. The only value of an accounting system is to provide meaningful information. The most elaborate financial statements and accounting systems in the world are useless unless the information is utilized. Therefore, before you choose the format, know what information is important to you.

Comparative Information

Comparative income statements provide information for the current reporting period along with some other income statement data. This other data usually reflects either the operating results from the same period of the preceding year, or, in a more sophisticated system, a budgeted or projected income statement for the same period.

Exhibit D illustrates the operating results of NuCorp compared to the results from the prior year.

Exhibit E illustrates the operating results of NuCorp, Inc. compared to the budget expectations for the same year.

Exhibit D – Operating Results

NuCorp, Inc.
Statement of Income
Two Years Ending December 31, 1996

	Year Ending Dec. 31, 1995	Year Ending Dec. 31, 1996
Sales	$1,200,000	$1,350,000
Cost of Sales	800,000	875,000
Gross Profit	400,000	475,000
Other Expenses:		
Marketing & Sales	140,000	175,000
General, Administrative	100,000	110,000
Research & Development	40,000	50,000
Total Other Expenses	280,000	335,000
Pre-tax Profit	120,000	140,000
Provision for Taxes	60,000	70,000
Net Income	$ 60,000	$ 70,000

The format in Exhibit D shows that the business has improved from one year to the next. The format can be expanded to show other years as well. For example, publicly held companies show the current year's results and the results of two preceding years to provide more meaningful information to shareholders.

Exhibit E – Current Information, Budget Expectations

NuCorp, Inc.
Actual and Budgeted Statement of Income
Year Ending December 31, 1996

	Budget	Actual
Sales	$1,200,000	$1,350,000
Cost of Sales	800,000	875,000
Gross Profit	400,000	475,000
Other Operating Expenses:		
Administrative Salaries	40,000	45,000
Rent Expense	12,000	15,000
Interest Expense	18,000	18,000
Legal & Accounting Expense	15,000	12,000
Office Supplies	5,000	6,000
Depreciation – Office Equipment	4,000	4,000
Janitorial Expense	3,000	4,000
Taxes & License	2,000	3,000
Miscellaneous Administration	1,000	3,000
Subcontract Labor – New Product	25,000	35,000
Research Materials	15,000	15,000
Sales Commissions	60,000	70,000
Advertising	30,000	45,000
Sales Promotion	15,000	15,000
Travel	8,000	15,000
Sales Brochures	7,000	5,000
Sales Salaries	20,000	25,000
Total Other Expenses	280,000	335,000
Pre-tax Profit	120,000	140,000
Provision for Taxes	60,000	70,000
Net Income	$ 60,000	$ 70,000

The format of Exhibit E also clearly shows the business expects to improve; additionally, it shows which expense categories should change from one year to the next. Notice that the comparative format can be used with any income statement format, presenting essentially the same information.

Additional information on income statement interpretation and analysis is presented in Chapter 3.

Examining Expenses

There is one more variation in income statement formatting that can be useful to many small businesses. This format involves increasing the information regarding individual products and product costs.

Product costs differ for a retail store and a manufacturing company. In a retail store, there is only one cost component — the cost of the product from the supplier. In a manufacturing environment there are three cost components.

Direct labor
This is the payroll cost for those employees whose only job is to make the product.

Direct materials
This is the cost of parts or materials which actually end up in the finished product.

Direct overhead
This includes all other costs incurred to manufacture a product, such as supervisors' salaries, building rent, utilities, and equipment depreciation.

The following examples illustrate the differences in cost of sale format for retail stores versus manufacturing environments.

Table 4 – Cost of Sales (retail store)

RetailCorp, Inc.
Statement of Income
Period Ending December 31, 1995

Sales	$1,200,000
Cost of Merchandise Sold	800,000
Gross Profit	$ 400,000

Table 4 illustrates the basic format for the cost of products sold for a retail store.

Table 5 – Cost of Sales (manufacturing company)

Manucorp, Inc.
Statement of Income
Period Ending December 31, 1995

Sales	$1,200,000
Cost of Sales:	
Direct Labor	300,000
Direct Materials	200,000
Direct Overhead	300,000
Gross Profit	$ 400,000

Table 5 illustrates the basic format for the cost of products sold for a manufacturing company. The additional value of this format can be seen in the following table, which assumes multiple products. Incidentally, the following formats for retail stores and manufacturing companies are useful for determining the profitability of various products or product lines.

Table 6 – Cost of Sales (multiproduct retail store)

RetailCorp, Inc.
Statement of Income
Period Ending December 31, 1995

	Product 1	Product 2	Product 3	All Products
Sales	$200,000	$700,000	$300,000	$1,200,000
Cost of Merchandise Sold	160,000	540,000	100,000	800,000
Gross Profit	$ 40,000	$160,000	$200,000	$ 400,000

Table 6 illustrates the format for a multiproduct retail store. Notice that Product 3 is the most profitable — Cost of Sale for Product 3 is 33%; for Product 2, 77%; and Product 1, 80%. This is the type of information an owner/manager needs.

Table 7 – Cost of Sales (multiproduct manufacturing company)

Manucorp, Inc.
Statement of Income
Period Ending December 31, 1995

	Product 1	Product 2	Product 3	All Products
Sales	$100,000	$600,000	$500,000	$1,200,000
Cost of Sales:				
Labor	50,000	150,000	100,000	300,000
Material	40,000	50,000	110,000	200,000
Overhead	60,000	140,000	100,000	300,000
Gross Profit	$ (50,000)	$260,000	$190,000	$ 400,000

Table 7 illustrates the format for a multiproduct manufacturing company. A considerable amount of information is conveyed in this presentation. In this example, Product 1 showed a $50,000 loss on sales of $100,000. Additional analysis shows that Product 2 is the most profitable.

Statements Must Provide Useful Information

The preceding identified the primary financial statements and their component parts. Additionally, a number of examples were shown to illustrate the range of formats which can be used for statement presentation. This format diversity exists to permit the business owner the freedom to design the financial statements which present meaningful information.

The desired information is obviously different for different types of businesses, as was shown for a retail company versus a manufacturing company, and for a single product business versus a multiple product business.

Chapter 3

Understanding Financial Statements

Know Your Financial Performance

Understanding financial statements is essential to understanding the financial performance of your business. Financial statements are necessary and extremely useful. However, the statements are only a start toward understanding where your business stands, where it is going, and how it is going to get there. You should study your business financial statements and learn to understand the relationship between some of the figures they represent. This section will explain various methods designed to help in assessing your company's financial performance.

Internal Benefits

Aside from external requirements — your bank, creditors, and others, as described later — you need to be aware of the valuable internal benefits of financial information presented in the financial statements. Internal benefits include measuring effectiveness of financial controls, profitability, safety, and the liquidity of your firm. We will analyze and discuss each of these factors to illustrate how financial statements are used to measure and understand a company's business performance.

Control

If your business is to survive, grow, and prosper — generate profits — it is important to have good financial controls as discussed in Chapter 5. One of the most important duties an owner or manager has is to keep the business' assets working efficiently and productively.

Small companies often think that "bigger is better" and allow their inventories, bank balances, and other key assets to grow beyond actual needs. For example: the sales manager wants a large finished goods inventory and easier credit terms against expected higher sales and the production manager wants newer and faster equipment and larger inventories in raw materials and supplies. Each will claim that these investments will make it easier for either sales or production to cut costs and meet delivery dates. The controller or financial manager wants large cash balances to meet company obligations and make his or her job easier. As you can see, the opportunity for unchecked spending is limitless without proper financial and cost controls!

The goal of management is to make certain that new or increased assets pay their way. Controlling these assets is the only way that management can be sure of earning reasonable profits from the business activity. For instance, by utilizing key ratios — which use elements from both profit and loss statement and the balance sheet — management can ascertain how effectively it is controlling the business' assets.

Both the balance sheet and income statement provide you with key financial information that will tell you how effectively you are managing and controlling the financial affairs of your business. Several analytic tools, including comparative analyses, plans, budges, and ratio analyses can assist you with measuring how well your company is doing. Each of these tools will be discussed in detail in later sections of this book.

To illustrate these basic points, we will make use of a hypothetical comparative profit and loss statement for NuCorp, Inc.

Exhibit F – Comparative Profit and Loss Statement

NuCorp, Inc.
Statement of Income
Years Ending December 31, 1995 and 1996

	Year Ending Dec. 31, 1995	Year Ending Dec. 31, 1996
Sales	$1,200,000	$1,350,000
Cost of Sales	800,000	955,000
Gross Profit	400,000	475,000
Other Expenses:		
Marketing & Sales	140,000	175,000
General, Administrative	100,000	110,000
Research & Development	40,000	50,000
Total Other Expenses	280,000	335,000
Pre-tax Profit	120,000	140,000
Provision for Taxes	60,000	70,000
Net Income	$ 60,000	$ 70,000

This Comparative Profit and Loss Statement clearly indicates that management is effectively controlling its day-to-day operations; sales have increased a modest 13% from 1995 to 1996, but profits have increased 17% over the previous year.

Based on the results, it is clear that NuCorp, Inc. management has kept a close watch over such expenses as cost of sales, resulting in a 19% increase of gross profits. We can also see that marketing and sales expenses increased, but the additional costs resulted in greater sales revenue. Additionally, a good indication of tight operation and cost controls is the relatively low increase of 10% in general and administrative expenses, which suggests a lean, productive support staff.

Understanding

A sound accounting system will provide you with timely and meaningful financial statements that can help you determine how effectively you are managing your business. Moreover, as demonstrated by a few examples of performance measurements, your company's financial statements are useful tools that allow you to exercise good controls.

Beyond the benefits of effective control and management, financial statements can also help you understand many important aspects of your business. For example, financial statements allow you to identify chief causes of problems, such as unnecessary increases in costs or investment. More importantly, once you see the causes of these problems, the information from financial statements will help you understand why they are occurring and how to remedy them. By comparing financial statements from one period to another or by comparing current financial statements to budgets, you can more readily spot problem areas and make timely management decisions before small problems become insurmountably large ones.

Improvement

As your business grows and prospers, there will probably be occasions when additional capital will be required for investment in facilities, equipment, or operations. You must be able to plan for these requirements and make intelligent decisions on how to best allocate the available resources.

There is a direct correlation between how well you understand financial statements and how well you understand the performance of your business. If you know how to "read" financial statements, you can answer such questions as:

- Will I need additional money?
- How much will I need, when will I need it, and where can I get it?
- What type of money, debt or equity, is best for me?
- Where can I get it?
- How much can I afford to pay for it?
- Am I collecting my receivables quickly enough?
- Do I have too much inventory?
- Can I take longer to pay my trade creditors?
- Am I controlling my production costs sufficiently?
- Am I controlling my administrative costs?

External Requirements

In addition to the need for timely financial statements, be aware that outsiders may also require this information. Banks, venture capitalists, leasing companies, insurance companies, suppliers, potential investors, and others all require these reports before granting a new loan or extending credit to or investing in your firm.

In some cases, regardless of how well you maintain your records and books, a creditor may require CPA-compiled or CPA-reviewed statements. Moreover, as a condition of a loan agreement, a creditor may request periodic statements in order to monitor the success of the business, to track the effectiveness of management, and to spot any potential problems that would affect your ability to make scheduled repayments or jeopardize the recovery of their loan.

Federal, state, and in some cases local governments require the filing of financial information for tax purposes. Failure to file timely and accurate tax returns can be fatal to a small business because of the severity of penalties imposed by the statutory agencies. Additionally, delinquent business taxpayers must pay interest on unpaid balances which, when combined with the penalties, can add up to substantial sums very quickly.

Insurance companies typically require access to financial records to determine the validity of losses claimed. The balance sheet, in such a case, is important in substantiating such claims as the cost of a fixed asset or the value of inventory. Insurance companies also perform payroll and gross receipts audits to determine workers' compensation and business liability insurance premiums.

Prospective buyers or investors will require financial statements revealing the worth and viability of your business before they decide to invest. They will want to see not only current financial statements but should request them for previous years to evaluate performance, growth rates, history of profitability, and other key business indicators. It is from this information that a sales price will be determined, negotiated, and agreed to by the interested parties.

The need for financial information by external parties is extensive but varies depending upon the nature, size, and type of business you operate. Publicly-held corporations — companies whose stock is listed and traded through the American, New York, and NASDAQ and other stock exchanges — are required to file annual and interim quarterly statements. Business disputes, litigations, and audits required by creditors or governmental agencies are other situations when your business financial statements may be required by outsiders.

Types of Analysis

As previously discussed, the balance sheet attempts to present an accurate and fair picture of the financial position of your business at the close of an accounting period.

The income statement also attempts to provide an accurate and fair picture of the operating results during an accounting (operating) period. These financial statements, if compiled according to generally accepted accounting principles, will be one of your most important sources of information. You can gain invaluable insight into your business from these statements through the use of analytical tools.

Several types of business performance analyses can be performed by using information from both the balance sheet and profit and loss statements. With simple mathematical calculations you can perform a variety of ratio, comparative, budgeting, and planning analyses that will allow you to determine just how well your company is performing. A brief description of these tools, and how to use them, follows.

Analytic Tools

Balance sheets and profit and loss statements, by themselves, are useful and necessary to measure your company's performance over an accounting period. Financial statements, whether prepared by you, a bookkeeper, or a CPA, take time to compile and can be costly. Get your money's worth out of them by learning to interpret the financial data contained within the statements. Study the relationship of figures presented in financial statements.

Comparative Analysis

Comparative analysis, utilizing your company's financial statements, can be performed on two general levels:

- For comparing your company's current performance against previous years' performance; and
- For comparing your company's performance against similar businesses in your industry, market, or geographic location.

The first type is easier to perform because you have all of the necessary data required to conduct the analysis.

This internal comparative analysis is done by comparing current and past operating results and financial performance. Through internal comparative analysis you can make comparisons by year, quarter, or month. Through internal comparative analysis you should be able to see, numerically or as a percentage, such things as sales increases or decreases, changes in cash balances, increases or decreases in liabilities, net worth, and specific expense accounts.

The second type of comparative analysis, comparing your company's performance to those of similar companies, is not quite as easy to conduct, since you will require external information.

To perform this analysis you must acquire trade and industry data from outside sources that compile such information. Industry and trade information can be obtained from your local business library, from trade associations, banks, brokerage firms, Dun & Bradstreet, Robert Morris & Associates, and other similar sources.

Ratio Analysis

Ratio analysis is one way to interpret just how well your company has done, which areas have improved over the past, which areas show weaknesses, and which need immediate management attention and action. Ratio indicators are comparative measurements expressed as ratios percentages or fractions — 3 to 1, 3:1, 300%, or 3/1.

The ratios provide clues for spotting and identifying both positive and negative trends. They also provide the means for you to compare your business' performance against the performance of similar businesses in your industry or market.

Ratios are useful in answering questions such as:

- Do I have too much inventory on hand?
- Are my customers paying me according to my credit policy?
- Do I have enough liquidity (cash) to meet immediate expenses?
- Is my business debt too high?
- What is the book value (worth) of my company?

As you perform ratio analysis, it is important to keep in mind a few important points.

- Businesses are different. There are many differences in businesses, even within those of similar size, nature of market, and locality. Each business uses different ways of recording and compiling certain line items of their financial statements. As a result, the figures for your company may not be identical to those for other businesses. However, there are enough similarities to allow you to make reasonable comparisons of your company's performance to that of your competition.

- Frequency of statement preparation. Ratios are computed for specific accounting periods and, unless they are prepared often, it may not be possible to gain meaningful insight into seasonal operating characteristics of your business.

- Ratios are not ends in themselves. Ratios are analytical tools that can help answer some of your financial questions and help you better understand how effectively your company is being managed. However, you can get these answers and insights only if you interpret them carefully.

- Financial statements are based on past performance. The ratios derived from these statements are useful in interpreting what has happened to date. They can also provide valuable clues to the future that will allow you to better prepare for problems and business opportunities that may present themselves. How you use these clues must be tempered by your best judgment about what is likely to happen in the future.

Ratios are among the easiest and most valuable ways to derive meaning from numbers. Ratio analysis gives you the ability to interpret the relationship between numbers on your balance sheets and profit and loss statements.

Ratio analysis is generally used to measure liquidity, profitability, and the relative safety or vulnerability of a company. By utilizing the NuCorp, Inc. Sample Income Statement and Sample Balance Sheet (exhibits G and H) as of December 31, 1996, samples of various business ratios can be illustrated.

Current ratio

The current ratio is one of the most commonly used tools to measure the financial strength of a company. This method measures the ability of a company to pay its current liabilities by using current assets only. The popular rule of thumb is that a 2:1 ratio is sufficient, but the higher the ratio, the better.

The formula for computing the current ratio follows.

$$\frac{\text{Total current assets}}{\text{Total current liabilities}}$$

Thus, the current ratio of NuCorp, Inc. is 1.63.

$$\frac{\$310,000}{\$190,000} = 1.63 \text{ (or 1.63 to 1)}$$

Is this a good current ratio? Should management of NuCorp, Inc. be satisfied with the company's ability to meet its current obligations? These questions generally can't be answered with a definitive "yes" or "no." If we hold with the rule of thumb that a current ratio of 2 to 1 is good, then the answer is "no."

However, whether a specific ratio is satisfactory depends on the nature of the business and characteristics of current assets and liabilities. There are some additional ratios that can help you make this determination.

Exhibit G – Sample Income Statement

NuCorp, Inc.
Statement of Income Period Ending December 31, 1996

	Period Ending Dec. 31, 1995	Period Ending Dec. 31, 1996
Sales	$1,200,000	$1,350,000
Materials Cost	800,000	955,000
Gross Profit	400,000	475,000
Other Operating Expenses:		
Administrative Salaries	40,000	45,000
Rent Expense	12,000	15,000
Interest Expense	18,000	18,000
Legal, Accounting Expense	15,000	12,000
Office Supplies	5,000	6,000
Depreciation – Office Equipment	4,000	4,000
Janitorial Expense	3,000	4,000
Taxes & License	2,000	3,000
Misc. Administration	1,000	3,000
Subcontract Labor – New Product	25,000	35,000
Research Materials	15,000	15,000
Sales Commissions	60,000	70,000
Advertising	30,000	45,000
Sales Promotion	15,000	15,000
Travel	8,000	15,000
Sales Brochures	7,000	5,000
Sales Salaries	20,000	25,000
Total Other Expenses	280,000	335,000
Pre-tax Profits	120,000	140,000
Provision for Taxes	60,000	70,000
Net Income	60,000	70,000

Exhibit H – Sample Balance Sheet

NuCorp, Inc.
Balance Sheet As of December 31, 1996

Assets

Current Assets:

Cash in Bank	$ 30,000	
Accounts Receivable	150,000	
Employees' Advances	10,000	
Inventory	100,000	
Prepaid Expenses	20,000	
Total Current Assets		$310,000

Fixed Assets:

Land & Building	200,000	
Office Equipment	20,000	
Machinery, Equipment	150,000	
Leasehold Improvements	30,000	
Accumulated Depreciation	(50,000)	
Total Fixed Assets		350,000

Other Assets:

Deposits	10,000	
Goodwill	50,000	
Total Other Assets		60,000
Total Assets		$720,000

Liabilities & Equity

Current Liabilities:

Accounts Payable	$100,000	
Payroll Taxes Payable	25,000	
Interest Payable	15,000	
Wages Payable	10,000	
Current Portion – Long-term Note Payable	40,000	
Total Current Liabilities		$190,000

Exhibit H – Sample Balance Sheet (continued)

Total Current Liabilities		$190,000
Long-term Liabilities:		
Mortgage Payable	150,000	
Bank Loan Payable	100,000	
Total Long-term Liabilities		250,000
Total Liabilities		$440,000
Shareholders' Equity:		
Common Stock	100,000	
Retained Earnings – Current	60,000	
Retained Earnings – Prior	120,000	
Total Shareholders' Equity		280,000
Total Liabilities & Equity		$720,000

Quick ratio – the acid test ratio

The quick ratio also measures the liquidity of a firm. The ratio indicates the ability of the company to pay its debt, its creditors, and other short-term obligations. A ratio of 1:1 or greater is desirable. Below is the formula for computing the quick ratio.

$$\frac{\text{Cash} + \text{Securities} + \text{Accounts receivable}}{\text{Current liabilities}}$$

By inserting the figures from NuCorp, Inc.'s balance sheet in Exhibit H into the formula, you can calculate its quick ratio.

$$\frac{\$180,000}{\$190,000} = .95 \text{ to } 1$$

The quick ratio is a much more meaningful liquidity measure than the current ratio. By eliminating inventories, it concentrates on very liquid assets — those that are immediately convertible to cash. It measures, in the absence of sales revenues, whether a company can meet its current obligations. In the case of NuCorp, Inc., we can see that with a ratio of .95 to 1, it would not be able to meet all of its current liabilities.

If NuCorp, Inc.'s management is concerned about its ability to meet current obligations should revenue be drastically reduced, they can take the following steps:

- Pay off some debt;
- Increase its current assets from new equity sources;
- Plow back profits rather than paying dividends;
- Convert noncurrent assets into current assets; or
- Convert inventory into accounts receivable, then into cash.

Average Collection Period

If your company currently sells its products on credit, or plans to do so in the future, the average collection period is a very important computation that you must perform. This ratio computes the average number of days it takes to collect accounts receivable. The average collection period ratio can be compiled from the balance sheet and the income statement.

First, determine the average daily sales by using this formula.

$$\frac{\text{Net yearly sales}}{365 \text{ days}} = \text{Average daily sales}$$

Then you can calculate the average collection period using this formula.

$$\frac{\text{Accounts receivable}}{\text{Average daily sales}} = \text{Average collection period}$$

By using these formulas, you can determine that NuCorp, Inc. made an average of $3,698 in sales per day and, with $150,000 in accounts receivable, that their average collection period was 41 days.

$$\frac{\$150,000}{\$3,698} = \text{41-day collection period}$$

By knowing the average collection period, it is possible to determine the quality of accounts receivable, the effectiveness of your credit policies, and how well your credit staff is handling the job of collecting on accounts. The fewer the days it takes to collect accounts receivable, the better your company's cash flow and the less risk of suffering from losses due to uncollectible or bad accounts, thus better profitability.

The average collection period or rule of thumb is that it should not exceed 1 1/3 times your credit terms. If NuCorp, Inc.'s policy is 30 days, its average collection period should not exceed 40 days. NuCorp's management should analyze why it is taking longer than the desired number of days to collect its receivables and make improvements. A review by management of an aging of Nucorp's accounts receivable would determine which customers are slow in paying, then by pursuing the collection of the overdue accounts could allow NuCorp to convert these receivables into cash.

Profitability Ratios

How do you know if your business is earning sufficient profit, given the amount of money invested in it? Could you put your money to work more efficiently in other places? The second most important financial management objective, after liquidity, is measuring how effectively your company is earning money. A number of ratios that do this have been developed. A few of them are presented below.

Return on equity

This ratio measures the return received on the capital invested in the business. The formula to compute this ratio is as follows:

$$\frac{\text{Net profit}}{\text{Equity}} = \text{Return on equity ratio}$$

The return on equity for NuCorp, Inc. for the period ending December 31, 1996 is as follows:

$$\frac{\$70,000}{\$280,000} = .25 \text{ or } 25 \text{ percent}$$

If you were to invest money in high interest-bearing certificates of deposit or bonds, you might receive a 7% return on equity invest. Therefore, a 25% return on equity is very good. In addition, don't ignore that your equity investment has also helped provide you with your salary and other benefits.

Tangible net worth

A variation of the net-profit/equity ratio uses tangible net worth. Tangible net worth is derived by subtracting from equity such assets as goodwill, research and development, patents, and other intangible assets. We can see a significant change in NuCorp's case if we subtract the $50,000 of goodwill on the balance sheet. The adjusted return on the adjusted net worth (equity) is 33 percent.

$$\frac{\$70,000}{\$210,000} = .33 \text{ or } 33 \text{ percent}$$

Gross profit margin

This ratio measures pricing effectiveness, ability to control inventories, and production efficiency at the gross profit level. The formula to compute this ratio follows.

$$\frac{\text{Gross profit}}{\text{Total sales}} = \text{Gross-profit-margin ratio}$$

The gross profit margin for NuCorp, Inc. for the period ending December 31, 1996 is 35 percent.

$$\frac{\$475,000}{\$1,350,000} = .35 \text{ or } 35 \text{ percent}$$

For NuCorp, Inc., it means that for every dollar of sales there is a 35% contribution that will go toward operating expenses and profit. Whether or not NuCorp, Inc. makes a profit depends on the ability of management to control operating expenses and maintain an adequate level of sales.

Net profit on sales

This ratio measures the difference between what your business takes in and what it spends to do business. The focus of this ratio is on two key business factors: control of operating expenses and pricing policies.

A decrease in net profit on sales might be due to a price reduction, made in hopes of increasing the sales volume. A reduction in the net-profit-on-sales ratio may also result if operating costs increased while prices remained the same.

To compute this ratio use the following formula.

$$\frac{\text{Net profit}}{\text{Net sales}} = \text{Net-profit-on-sales ratio}$$

Nucorp, Inc.'s net profit on sales ratio is 5 percent.

$$\frac{\$70,000}{\$1,350,000} = .05 \text{ or } 5 \text{ percent}$$

For every dollar of sales, the business is making five cents.

While this ratio can be used to show changes in your business from period to period, its usefulness actually comes into play when comparing figures with those of similar businesses.

Return on assets

Several types of ratios are also used to determine the profitability of a business. Most common among these is the return-on-assets ratio.

$$\frac{\text{Net profit}}{\text{Total assets}} = \text{Return-on-assets ratio}$$

The return on assets of NuCorp, Inc. is 9.7 percent.

$$\frac{\$70,000}{\$720,000} = 9.7 \text{ percent}$$

This ratio measures how effectively a company manages its assets to generate a profit.

Safety Ratios

Safety ratios are used to determine the company's exposure to risk; specifically, to what degree the company's business debt is protected. We will look at three commonly used ratios to help you evaluate and understand how you can measure safety.

Debt-to-net-worth ratio

This ratio measures the relationship between the capital invested by owners (net worth) and funds borrowed from creditors (debt). The higher the ratio, the greater the risk to a creditor. A lower ratio means your company is more financially stable and could probably borrow additional funds now or in the future. Conversely, if the debt-to-net-worth ratio is too low, it may mean that you are too conservative and are not utilizing the business assets efficiently.

Looking at NuCorp, Inc.'s Sample Balance Sheet for the period ending December 31, 1996, the debt-to-net-worth ratio can be calculated as follows:

$$\frac{\text{Debt (total liabilities)}}{\text{Net worth (equity)}} = \text{Debt-to-net-worth ratio}$$

$$\frac{\$440,000}{\$280,000} = 1.57 \text{ percent}$$

Is Nucorp's debt too high in relation to the equity invested? It would seem that NuCorp, Inc. might have difficulty borrowing much more in the short term without additional equity capital injections.

Times interest earned

The times-interest-earned ratio measures your company's ability to make its interest payments. Moreover, it is also an indicator of your company's ability to take on more debt. Obviously, the higher the ratio, the greater the ability of your company to borrow more.

This is the formula for calculating this ratio.

$$\frac{\text{Earnings before interest and taxes}}{\text{Interest charges}} = \text{Times-interest-earned ratio}$$

From NuCorp, Inc.'s Sample Income Statement the times-interest-earned ratio is 8.78 times.

$$\frac{\$158,000}{\$18,000} = 8.78 \text{ times}$$

In this instance, it is apparent that NuCorp's management has considerable flexibility to borrow more funds if it wishes because of the company's ability to pay more interest to potential creditors. Notice that the debt-to-net-worth ratio implies that the company should not incur additional debt, yet the times-interest-earned ratio implies the company can incur additional debt. Sometimes different ratios are contradictory.

Total debt to total assets

This ratio compares both short-term and long-term liabilities to total assets and shows what proportion of funds has been provided by all creditors. The formula for computing total-debt-to-total-assets follows.

$$\frac{\text{Total debt (liabilities)}}{\text{Total assets}} = \text{Total-debt-to-total-assets ratio}$$

Using NuCorp, Inc.'s Sample Balance Sheet for the period ending December 31, 1996, you can calculate this ratio.

$$\frac{\$190,000 + \$250,000}{\$720,000} = .61$$

Other Common Balance Sheet Ratios

There are a considerable number of other ratios used to analyze a balance sheet. Among these are inventory turnover and average payment period.

Inventory turnover

This ratio measures the number of times a year your inventory is converted into sales. It is determined by this formula.

$$\frac{\text{Cost of materials}}{\text{Average inventory}} = \text{Inventory-turnover ratio}$$

In the case of Nucorp, Inc., this is calculated for 1996, where inventory on December 31, 1995 was $80,000.

$$\frac{\text{Cost of materials}}{(1995 \text{ inventory } + 1996 \text{ inventory}) \times 1/2}$$

or

$$\frac{\$875,000}{(\$80,000 + \$100,000) \times \frac{1}{2}} = 9.72 \text{ times per year}$$

This can also be expressed in terms of number of days.

$$\frac{\text{Number of days in period}}{\text{Inventory turnover}} = \text{Inventory-turnover ratio}$$

$$\frac{365}{9.72} = 37.55 \text{ days}$$

This ratio shows that Nucorp, Inc. converted its inventory into sales approximately every 38 days during 1996.

Average payment period

Average payment period demonstrates the period of credit which you obtain from your creditors, or more simply, the number of days it takes you to pay your bills. This is the formula.

$$\frac{\text{Average accounts payable}}{\text{Total expenses (excluding payroll, interest, rent, depreciation, and taxes}} \times \text{Number of days in period}$$

The reason for excluding expense items such as payroll, interest, rent, depreciation, and taxes is that these types of expenses are not usually recorded in accounts payable.

In the case of Nucorp, Inc., where accounts payable on December 31, 1995 was $90,000 and total expenses — excluding payroll, interest, rent, depreciation, and taxes — amounted to $649,000, the average payment period was 53.43 days.

$$\frac{(1995 + 1996 \text{ accounts payable}) \times \frac{1}{2}}{\text{Total expenses, less non-accounts payable items}} \times \text{Number of days in period}$$

or

$$\frac{(\$90,000 + \$100,000) \times \frac{1}{2}}{\$649,000} \times 365 = 53.43 \text{ days}$$

This means that Nucorp, Inc. took an average of nearly 54 days to pay its trade creditors during 1996.

Percentage of Sales

Most of the above ratios are derived from the balance sheet. The most common ratio derived strictly from the income statement is the percentage-of-sales ratio. This consists of each expense item in the income statement being expressed as a percentage of the value of sales in the income statement. A detailed example can be found in Appendix II, but here is a simple example.

	Amount	Percentage of Sales
Sales	$50,000	100.0
Cost of Sales	35,173	70.3

In this example, each dollar of sales yields 29.7 cents toward profit and for paying other costs of the business after paying 70.3 cents of direct costs of sales. You can then compare this result to the past business performance and determine if the trend is changing — if it is, you may want to find out why.

You may also compare this result to the results of other companies to see how your business is doing relative to competitors in the same field. You can obtain the information to do this from published sources such as Robert Morris Associates, Dun and Bradstreet, trade publications, and the annual reports of public companies. The calculation and consideration of the results of a percentage-of-sales analysis is extremely useful in helping you understand the dynamics of your business. It is also critical in helping you prepare a budget for use in your business planning.

Financing Cycle

Every business has a series of cycles. Each cycle involves the action and time required from start to completion of a discrete part of the business operation. For instance, the sale cycle commences with taking an order and ends with collecting cash from the customer.

The financing cycle is a quick calculation which will tell you roughly how much liquidity is needed for normal business operations. The input for this calculation comes from some of the ratios discussed earlier in this section.

This is the formula for calculating the financing cycle.

Inventory turnover days
+ Average accounts receivable collection period
= Days to convert inventory into cash
− Average payment period
= Financing cycle

In the case of Nucorp, Inc., this would be as follows:

38 Inventory turnover days
+ 41 Average collection in period
= 79 Days to convert inventory into cash
− 54 Average payment period
= 25 Financing cycle

This indicates that Nucorp, Inc. needs to have cash balances that are able to pay for 25 days' expenses at any period of time. As Nucorp, Inc.'s business continues to grow, it is likely that the dollar amount of cash reserves required will increase, even if the financing cycle length remains at 25 days.

Comparisons Can Be Valuable

Ratios, while useful, will not provide you with automatic solutions to your business orientation or financial problems. Ratios are only tools for measuring the performance of your business. It is the use to which you put them that will determine their real value.

Compare your ratios with average ratios for various types of businesses. Compare your ratios to those of similar businesses. Additionally, compare your own ratios for several successive months or years. Look for trends, especially unfavorable trends, that may cause problems for your business.

Budgeting

For many business people, budgeting is the core of planning the future of their business. Budgets can range from very simple to extremely complex.

The most common example of a budget is what most people do with their personal income and checking account. You probably already do this, even if only mentally. This type of budget tends to be determined by fixed income (salary) and fixed expenses, such as mortgage payments, automobile payments, and food.

Most people go through this budgeting exercise to determine how much they have to spend on discretionary items such as entertainment and vacations. For many small businesses the budgeting process is similar — the aim is to determine when you can afford new equipment or a new advertising campaign.

Budgeting for businesses can achieve much more than determining what it takes to get the ending cash balance to equal zero! Many business owners and managers do not understand the real value of budgeting. In fact, budgeting or any form of planning is ignored by too many small business owners. This is unfortunate since the business owner or manager who plans for the future and budgets accordingly has two distinct advantages over their competition. The owner or manager knows where the business is headed and has a guide to get there by understanding the economics of the business.

What then is the budgeting process? Simplistically, it is a process of predicting what will happen to your business over the next 12 months and tracking the results.

What is the source of budget data? It begins with the historic information provided by your accounting system. The general ledger provides annual historic information for every activity of your business.

Effect of Budgeting on Expenses

The primary focus of budgeting is on expenditures. There are four types of expenses.

Fixed costs

No matter how your sales may increase or decrease, some expenses, called fixed costs, remain static. Examples of these costs include rent, equipment leases, and insurance.

Variable costs

Some other expenses, called variable costs, vary directly in relation to sales. Examples of these are sales commissions and the cost of goods sold (cost of sales).

Semivariable costs

These are expenses that remain fairly static for a range of sales, then increase or decrease to another static amount. The best example of a semivariable cost is salaries. Salary expense tends to be similar from week to week; however, if sales increased dramatically, you may have to hire additional people. This type of cost is also sometimes called a step function cost.

Discretionary costs

The amount and timing of this type of expense is usually determined by the business owner or manager. An example of this type is sales promotion costs. These are usually incurred to support and stimulate sales, based on a sales plan. The sales promotion costs are also expected to have an effect on sales volume. Therefore, when budgeting for discretionary costs, it is important to remember the anticipated effect on sales and the variable costs which fluctuate with changes in sales volume.

Effect of Budgeting on Sales

In budgeting it is relatively easy to predict what your business costs will be and when they will occur. You have a wealth of historic information in your accounting system as a source of data. Sales are not as easy to predict, but historic information in your accounting system can be of assistance. This information will tell you various things, including:

- The seasonality of your sales,
- The nature of your customer base,
- Your base sales levels, and
- The historic effect of your sales promotions.

Once you have reviewed the historic information, you know what has affected sales in the past. This base knowledge, combined with your understanding of your market and competitors and independent estimates of future sales expectations for your industry, puts you in a position to budget sales.

The budgeting process is simply a prediction for each transaction account of what costs should be to achieve an anticipated sales level. These costs and sales should be itemized on a monthly basis.

Every transaction account in your accounting system should have a monthly budgeted amount. This is your expectation of what that cost, revenue, and balance sheet item should be at the end of the month.

How to Use a Budget

Once you have created a budget, what do you do with it? You should compare, on a monthly basis, the actual results in your financial statements to your budgeted amounts. This will tell you how change is affecting your business and will allow you to use your budget process as a control over your operations.

For instance, suppose you budgeted $5,000 for merchandise costs for the month but your actual statement of income shows that $8,000 was spent. Since you have a benchmark to measure against, you can investigate the cause of the discrepancy to determine whether there is a problem. It may be that sales were much higher than originally budgeted — your merchandise costs would therefore be higher. If sales were within budget, you may have product quality control problems or a theft problem.

Having prepared a budget, you are now in a position to respond to change. The budget will assist you in planning for the future of your business.

Budgeting is also a process that will provide you with a solid understanding of the economics of your business and the dynamics of the marketplace in which your business competes. Finally, it provides you with a control function which can point out possible problem areas and allow you to more effectively manage your business.

Many businesses do not budget. They should. Any business owner or manager who does not go through a budgeting process is operating his or her business on intuition without really understanding where that business is likely to go.

Planning

If you do not know where you want to go, you will never get there. You will get somewhere, but you may not be too happy about where you end up.

Planning is a function that is ignored nearly as often as budgeting. The cause is usually ignorance of the process and, in this case, ignorance probably will not be bliss.

Planning is a systematic process that requires the business owner to understand the financial ramifications of his or her business. In its broadest sense, planning means projecting future business sales and expenses to determine future profitability or viability. In order to plan effectively, you have to understand the cost structure of the business. You must know your production costs, the levels of general and administrative costs necessary to support the business, and the marketing and sales costs necessary to achieve your desired sales level.

In short, you must understand the microeconomics of your business. Do not be intimidated — this only means you have to know your monthly rent, how much you pay for your merchandise or components, how much mark-up you can add to determine sales price, how many employees are needed and how much to pay them, and so on. This is vital information! The business owner who does not understand the financial implications of his or her business will probably fail.

Proper planning means effective management. Planning can be formal or informal, short-term or long-term. It can be used to assess the future of the entire company, or to assess a specific project or business investment, such as an equipment purchase, expansion, or advertising campaign.

All major corporations plan for the future. Whereas corporations are ultimately concerned with the future value of their stock in the stock market, the small business person has a different focus: How much cash can I take out of the business? Thus, the subtle virtue of planning is that it can tell you how to manage your business.

The first thing to do is ask yourself some key questions:

- What are your goals for the next five years?
- Do you want to expand to multiple locations?
- Do you want to be a millionaire?
- Do you want to be acquired by another company?
- Do you want to acquire other companies?
- Do you want to build a family business which can be passed on to future generations?
- Do you just want to maintain what you already have?

All of these goals have financial ramifications for the business. Understanding these ramifications will allow you to manage your company in the desired direction. Examples of steps taken to attain certain goals include:

- Increasing your business' net worth by drawing a smaller salary. This could result in a higher sale price when the business is sold.
- Accepting a lower profit margin to increase customer support. By building a strong reputation for price, you may be able to more easily expand into new locations.
- Reinvesting frequently in the plant or in equipment. By maintaining high-quality facilities and a large production capability, you may build a company which will last for generations.

These examples are somewhat simplistic, because several businesses strategies will support different business goals. Nevertheless, the important idea is that by planning, defining goals, and modifying business management, you can determine where you are going — and you just might get there!

Planning requires creativity. It begins with defining goals. Once you have defined your goals, it is time to be creative. First consider what you do in your business. What works and what doesn't work? Then, with your goal in mind, think of every business tactic you believe will assist you in attaining that goal.

Do not limit yourself. The creative person will think of as many tactics as possible. You will need more than a couple of actions to avoid going out of business. No possible action is too absurd to consider! Planning is also considering! Once you have identified several thousand possible tactics, analyze them. Every one of them.

Planning is also analysis! This is where budgeting and a basic understanding of the economics of your business are important. Analysis in a business sense basically means asking, "What is the effect of this activity on my balance sheet and income statement?" Analyze every possible tactic from the financial standpoint of how much an action will cost versus what you stand to gain from it.

As you read in previous sections, every physical event in business has an effect on the balance sheet or income statement — there is a debit or a credit entered in your accounting system for every event. It will show up on your statements, either as a positive or a negative. Obviously you will then want to choose a positive action, hopefully the most financially positive action. So, planning is also choosing!

Once you have defined goals, identified possible courses of action, and analyzed the financial ramifications of each alternative, it is time to select the most beneficial action or combination of actions. This is why you should plan. By choosing the most beneficial action, you can have a positive effect on your business.

By setting goals, identifying various business tactics, and analyzing and choosing the most positive courses of action, you will have an advantage over much of your competition. You will also be effectively managing your business, the same way that most successful businesspeople do!

Chapter 4

Be Your Own Bookkeeper

Accounting Is Not Difficult

One of the greatest misconceptions in business is the perception that accounting is difficult. It is not difficult! The basis for most "bean-counter" and "bookkeeper" jokes is the fact that few people in business understand accounting. The unfortunate reality for business owners who do not understand the basic principles of accounting is that they will not understand the underlying economics of a business.

It can be argued that understanding the underlying economics of a business is the most important skill a business owner or manager can possess. If costs are out of control or pricing is inadequate, no amount of sales, merchandising, or production skills can compensate. The business will fail. This is not to say that a business owner or manager must perform the accounting work themselves; rather, an owner has the responsibility to understand "what the numbers mean."

Chapters 2 and 3 explained financial statements. Understanding these sections will provide a business owner with a reasonable basis for financial control of the business. The purpose of this section is to provide sufficient information for the reader to develop an understanding of accounting tasks. Additionally, with some help from an accountant, the reader should be able to perform his or her own accounting work.

It is not necessary that a business owner perform the accounting function. In many cases it is desirable that the business owner not perform the accounting function. In most situations, a person starts a business because of particular skills or product knowledge; it is in the best interests of the owner to spend as much time and effort as possible on that function. Time spent on accounting, when the owner could otherwise be generating higher sales or better production, can be detrimental to the business.

In many situations, a business owner can make time available, but chooses not to. This is a mistake. It costs a business, at minimum, a couple thousand dollars per year for somebody else to do the work — a significant savings if the owner can do it. More importantly, it costs the intimate knowledge of the business that is gained from processing all of the documents — invoices, checks, and other transaction documents — generated by business activity.

Accounting or bookkeeping — these terms can be used interchangeably — is a symbolic function. It describes and values "transactions." A transaction is an event that occurs in a business day: a customer purchasing the product; an advertisement placed in the local media; a delivery of products or supplies; a payment made on a loan; the receipt or payment of a check for any business purpose; and any other action that occurs in the daily performance of a business.

Whereas the accounting layman will describe the event in physical terms — the salesman bought lunch for a potential customer — the accountant will systematically symbolize and value that event. The following information will explain how that symbolizing and valuing process works.

To reiterate, accounting is not difficult! Do not be intimidated by something that is incorrectly perceived as being difficult. The reward for not being intimidated is cash — money you do not have to pay to an outside accountant and increased profits from a better run business.

Three Concepts

Before learning how to perform the accounting function, you should become familiar with three new concepts: double-entry, debits and credits, and transaction accounts. These concepts relate to the symbolic function of accounting — symbolizing and systemizing the daily events of a business.

Double entry

Double entry is described precisely by a law of physics, "For every action there is an equal and opposite reaction." In physics, every cause has an effect — a force pushes and something moves.

In accounting, every event has two effects: money is given and something is received in return. All business events are an exchange of one thing for another. Therefore, in the accounting function, the result is that when an event is recorded, it is recorded twice: once as a positive "action," and once — in an equal amount — as a negative "reaction" or response. This concept helps make accounting easy.

Since each event is recorded two times, once as a positive and once as a negative, if you subtract the negative from the positive, the result should equal zero. If the net (positive minus negative) does not equal zero, a mistake has been made.

Debits and credits

Debits and credits refer to the "positive" and "negative" actions mentioned above. They are the terms used to record an event. Each event is recorded twice — once as a debit and once as a credit. An entry in the same amount — as a debit and a credit — is the basis of "double-entry" accounting. For example, if a customer purchases a product from your business for cash, the following entry will be made:

- Debit – Cash received
- Credit – Sales (product sold)

How do you know what to debit and what to credit? The answer to this question is the only complicated part of describing accounting functions.

What determines whether an entry should be a debit or credit? It depends upon the nature of the account, and whether the event (transaction) will increase or decrease that account. The following table shows different types of accounts and the effect of a debit and credit upon it.

Table 8 – The Effect of Debits and Credits on Accounts

Account type*	Normal balance	To increase account enter as a . . .	To decrease account enter as a . . .
Asset	Debit	Debit	Credit
Liability	Credit	Credit	Debit
Capital	Credit	Credit	Debit
Income	Credit	Credit	Debit
Expense	Debit	Debit	Credit

* Typical Asset = Cash
   Typical Liability = Accounts payable
   Typical Capital = Common stock
   Typical Income = Sales
   Typical Expenses = Rent and supplies

The following examples of event and effect illustrate the concepts outlined in Table 8:

Event	Effect
Customer purchases product from store for $50	Cash is increased, sales are increased. Debit (cash) and credit (sales)
You pay landlord the monthly rent of $900	Cash is decreased, expenses are increased. Credit (cash) and debit (expenses)
You purchased office supplies on account from a stationery store	Accounts payable is increased, office expense is increased. Credit (accounts payable) and debit (expenses)

Observe that in each case, there is a debit and a credit. Also note that, in two cases, there were two increases and in the other there was an increase and a decrease. It does not matter whether there are increases or decreases. The important point is that there has to be a debit and a credit. Learn Table 8 and refer to it as often as needed throughout this book.

Transaction account

The final symbolic concept to understand is the transaction account. A transaction, as mentioned earlier, is an event which occurs during the business day. These transactions are shortened, much like shorthand is used to save space and increase speed, into a one- or two-word description. Paying the landlord the monthly rent is simply known as "rent expense" — rent, for obvious reasons and expense because it is a cost of doing business — as opposed to an asset or a liability. Similarly, any cost of doing business is called an expense: insurance expense, rent expense, payroll expense, office expense, and so on. These represent the physical acts of paying for your insurance, paying your landlord, paying your employee(s), and purchasing office supplies. These are transaction accounts.

The next step in understanding transaction accounts is to pre-identify typical transactions your business performs and place them in a logical, numbered sequence. This is called a chart of accounts. The purpose of the chart of accounts is to simplify your workload. The accounts are grouped and numbered according to whether they represent assets, liabilities, capital, or expenses. Table 9 is a description of a chart of accounts. The specific accounts used are representative of typical transactions, but are not inclusive. You should create and use your own chart of accounts, depending upon your normal transactions. Also, the numbering system shown in the example below is common but not absolute — you may use any numbering system you wish, or no numbering system at all.

Table 9 – Chart of Accounts

Account number	Account description
100	Cash in Bank (general account)
101	Petty Cash
110	Accounts Receivable
111	Advances to Employees
120	Inventory (raw materials)*
121	Inventory (work-in-process)*
122	Inventory (finished goods)*
130	Prepaid Insurance
140	Building
141	Accumulated Depreciation (building)
142	Machinery and Equipment
143	Accumulated Depreciation (machinery and equipment)
144	Leasehold Improvements
145	Accumulated Depreciation (leasehold)
170	Rental Deposits
180	Other Assets
185	Goodwill
200	Accounts Payable
210	Payroll Tax Payable (federal)
211	Payroll Tax Payable (state)
215	Sales Tax Payable
220	Interest Payable
230	Loans Payable (current portion)

Account number	Account description
240	Other Current Liabilities
260	Bank Loan Payable
265	Mortgage Payable
300	Owner's Capital
310	Retained Earnings (prior years)
315	Retained Earnings (current year)
400	Sales**
500	Cost of Sales***
600	Advertising Expense
605	Depreciation Expense (building)
606	Depreciation Expense (machinery and equipment)
610	Insurance Expense
615	Interest Expense
620	Janitorial Expense
625	Leased Equipment
630	Miscellaneous Expense
635	Office Supplies Expense
640	Postage Expense
645	Rent Expense
650	Travel Expense
655	Utility Expense

* In a retail store, these accounts might be classified as Merchandise Inventory. There can be as many accounts as you want — one account may contain all of your product; two accounts can be used to show two major product lines; or many accounts can be used to help control inventory.

** Sales can be treated the same way as Merchandise Inventory — one account can be used for all products, or multiple accounts can be used for each specific product or product line. This decision should be based on the following rule of thumb: "If I take the trouble to gather this information, will I utilize it?" Gather only data that you will use.

*** Cost of Sales can be one account (in retail), or many accounts (in manufacturing). Examples include the following:

Retail	500	Merchandise Cost
Manufacturing	500	Direct Labor
	510	Direct Materials
	520	Direct Overhead

Manufacturing costs relate to the direct costs of producing the product sold. Manufacturing costs consist of the following:

- Labor. Employees who make the product.

- Raw materials. Materials used in manufacturing the product.

- Overhead. All other costs involved in manufacturing the product, including rent expense, equipment leasing expense, utilities, supervisors' salaries, wasted supplies — any cost incurred in making the product, that is not considered direct labor or materials.

Another way of looking at the chart of accounts is illustrated.

Table 10 – Chart of Accounts and Category Numbers

Account number	Account description
100–149	Current assets
150–179	Fixed assets
180–199	Other assets
200–250	Current liabilities
251–299	Long-term liabilities
300–399	Capital stock
400–499	Sales
500–599	Cost of sales
600–699	Marketing and sales expenses
700–799	General and administrative expenses
800–899	Other income and other expenses

The chart of accounts is always presented in this order; assets are listed first, followed by liabilities, capital, income, and expenses in that order. In listing assets, current assets are listed first, followed by fixed assets, and other assets.

In summary, the accounting system is a double-entry system, with each accounting entry consisting of a debit and a credit. The actual entry of these debits and credits will occur using transaction accounts.

The Accounting Cycle

Prior to going into the specifics of how to "run" a set of books, this section will outline the general tasks that must be learned. This preliminary overview of the entire process should make the following sections easier to understand.

The Accounting Cycle

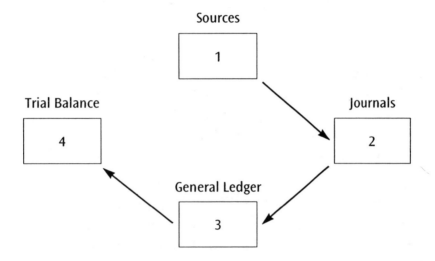

1. Sources: Pieces of paper (checks and invoices).
2. Enter each transaction into the proper journal.
3. Transfer (post) all journal totals to a general ledger.
4. List all general ledger accounts in a trial balance.

Entries

Accounting describes and quantifies all of the events or transactions which occur in a business. There are two situations in which an accounting entry should be made. Both of these situations are known as sources or source documents.

- Whenever a check, invoice, or purchase order is sent or received by the company; and

- When certain non-paper transactions must be entered at the end of an accounting period. These non-paper transactions can include: recognizing the depreciation of equipment for the period; recognizing interest expense that has not been paid but has accrued — for example, you know that more money is owed but no additional invoices have been sent; or recognizing other "accrued expenses" for which you have not received an invoice.

You enter a transaction following the receipt of a source document. An entry is made into a journal, remembering to enter both a debit and a credit. A number of different journals can be used.

Once all source documents are entered for an accounting period, it is time to total all transactions. This is done by transferring, or posting, the dollar totals from the journals to a general ledger. The general ledger will accumulate all activity for all of the transaction accounts in one place and facilitate totaling each transaction account.

After totaling the accounts, the sum is posted to a working trial balance sheet — a columned sheet which contains the entire chart of accounts and is organized into a balance sheet section and an income statement section. In the process of transferring from the general ledger to the working trial balance sheet, you have prepared both the balance sheet and the income statement.

The accounting cycle is explained in summary in Table 11.

Table 11 – Events and Responses in the Accounting Cycle

Event	Response
Received or sent a piece of paper	Enter debit and credit in journal
Entered all pieces of paper in journals	Post from journals to general ledger
Posted all journals to general ledger	Post all transaction account sums to working trial balance sheet
Posted all transaction accounts from general ledger to working trial balance sheet	Transfer balance sheet and income statement data to whatever format you use for statements

Timing Variables for Accounting Tasks

There is one additional issue which should be mentioned prior to presenting specific examples of the accounting cycle. The frequency with which accounting work should be performed depends upon several variable factors.

The number of transactions

If few checks and invoices are sent or received in a month, the work can be performed infrequently — weekly, biweekly, or even monthly. The larger the volume of transactions, the more frequently the work must be performed.

Assume that, as a novice, it takes approximately one minute to enter each transaction — debit and credit — into the journals. If you write 50 checks and receive 100 invoices per month, there are 150 transactions to be entered, or "booked," per month. With this volume of work, it would only take $2\frac{1}{2}$ hours to enter all of the transactions. Add an additional four hours for payroll calculations — see Payroll Schedules later in this chapter — three hours for posting from the journals to the general ledger, and four hours for posting from the general ledger to the working trial balance sheet. The entire accounting cycle can be completed in about 14 hours.

If your business has more (or fewer) transactions, you can approximate the number of hours required. Don't feel badly if it takes a bit longer at first.

The time the owner or manager has to perform the work

In most cases, the owner is most valuable to the business working with customers or helping to produce the product. If you are already working 60 or 70 hours per week, you may not have the energy or the inclination to regularly perform the accounting function. In that case, you should perform the work on a frequency based on the next variable.

The value of the information to the owner/manager

If you are not using financial information to assist in management of the business, there is no compelling reason to perform the accounting function frequently. In this "worst case," it would be reasonable to prepare financial statements only once a year — for the tax authorities. If you are interested in or able to use the accounting information to manage your business, the financial statements should be prepared more often, preferably monthly or at least quarterly.

For more information about the benefits derived from using financial information see Chapter 3, Understanding Financial Statements.

Original Entries

Original entries are made into the accounting system through the use of journals. These entries are generated from two sources: source documents and recurring transactions.

Source Documents

These documents verify the information in your accounting system — which is why they are called "source" documents — and are of vital interest to your company. They include:

- Checks written
- Checks received
- Cash paid out
- Cash received

- Invoices sent
- Invoices received — payment obligations
- Purchase orders sent to a vendor or supplier — when product is received
- Payment stubs — such as loan repayment booklets and lease payments

A logical filing system should be established and all documents that support — verify accounting entries — the financial statements should be filed logically to be available during the reporting period.

The importance of these source documents is external. If you should ever be audited by the Internal Revenue Service or other tax authorities, you will need the source documents to support your financial statements. Also, if you want to sell your business or go public, any reasonably sophisticated purchaser will want to at least review your accounting system or, if the purchase price is substantial, the purchaser will retain the services of an accounting firm and formally audit your books and records.

Whenever an invoice is paid, you should write "Paid" and the date of payment on the invoice, then initial the invoice before placing it in the permanent file. Whenever you receive a check from a customer, you should photocopy the check and deposit slip prior to the deposit, then place the photocopies in a permanent file. This record is a superior audit trail and can occasionally resolve potential disputes with customers.

Recurring Transactions

There are several transactions that do not have paper "sources." They include:

- Noncheck bank charges or bank transfers, either into or out of your bank account — these will appear on your bank statement, but may not have deposit or charge receipts for your records.
- Depreciation charges you make on a periodic basis. See Depreciation in this chapter.
- Additional interest charges which may be owed on leases or loans. These are accrued expenses.

- Payroll withholding and other payroll related expenses. See Payroll Schedules in this chapter.

- Expenses you know have been incurred, such as telephone or utilities, but have not been invoiced by your supplier at the time you prepare your financial statements. These are accrued expenses.

- Any other cost of doing business for which you have not received an invoice, such as bonuses or commissions earned, but not yet paid. These are accrued expenses.

Since there are no pieces of paper to support these transactions, they must be created internally. For example, payroll-related charges are the most frequently occurring transactions. A payroll schedule should be prepared for every payroll paid. This schedule should show the withholding of all federal, state, local, and other deductions made from each employee's wage or salary. See example in Payroll Schedules.

This payroll schedule should be included in your records as support for entries made for these transactions. Similarly, if there are bonuses or commissions accrued, a schedule detailing the amount should be made and included in your audit trail.

A final note on nonpaper sources: all of the accounting entries for these transactions will be entered in a general journal. The support for entries which do not have a schedule backing them up should consist of a simple handwritten note under the actual entry. See Exhibit I below.

Using Journals

There are two basic types of journals: two-column and multi-column or spreadsheet. Two columns is the minimum because this is double-entry accounting, with each entry requiring a debit and a credit entry in the same dollar amount. A multicolumn journal is useful for cash and credit transactions. Multicolumn spreadsheets should be used for cash and purchasing journals.

Two-column Journal

Exhibit I below illustrates a two-column journal and its appropriate column headings.

Exhibit I – Two-column Journal

General Journal
May 31, 19XX

Date	Description	Debit	Credit
5/31	Depreciation Expense Accumulated Depreciation *(To record depreciation expense* *for equipment for the month of* *May)*	725.00	725.00
5/31	Commission Expense Commissions Payable *(To record commission expense* *for commissions earned, but* *not paid in May per attached* *commission schedule)*	900.00	900.00

The two-column journal should only be used as the general journal and the general ledger. The heading at the top of the page should always identify the specific journal and show the time period represented by that journal. The column headings shown should always be used. The left column should show the date for which the entry is being made. This is not necessarily the date you are actually performing the work. Instead, the date entered should represent the time period for which the transaction occurred — if on June 8 you are performing the accounting work for the month of May, the appropriate date to enter in the date column is May 31. The wide column to the right of the date column should give a description of the transaction — for instance, the name of the transaction account describing the physical event which has occurred, such as: Rent Expense. The next column should be the debit entry, with the last column showing the credit entry. Underneath each transaction entry, there should be a written explanation of why the entry was made — a necessity when you use a manual system.

In Exhibit I, the first transaction recorded (or entered) is the depreciation expense during the month of May for equipment used in the business. There is no schedule for this entry, so the note is the "source" of the entry.

A fixed asset schedule can be used as the source. This schedule details each piece of equipment purchased by the business, the date purchased, the original cost, the number of months over which it will be depreciated, and the monthly depreciation in dollars. This detailed information can be left in the general file for review, and need not be appended or attached to the journal. See Depreciation for an example.

The second transaction entry is for commissions earned by sales personnel. There should be a schedule which identifies each person, and the amount earned. This schedule, which should be attached to the general journal, provides the audit trail (verifies the entry) for this transaction.

Remember, when using a manual system, all entries in the general journal should include a descriptive explanation for the entry. These descriptive explanations may not be necessary when using an automated system.

Multi-column (Spreadsheet) Journal

The multi-column spreadsheet should be used for all other journals. Whereas the general journal can be used for any type of transaction, all other journals are used for a specific transaction type — the cash disbursements journal is used only when the business issues a check, the cash receipts journal is used only when the business receives cash or checks from customers, and so on.

Illustrated in Exhibit J is a multi-column spreadsheet with sample column headings.

Since other journals are specific to a transaction, there is only one debit or one credit — depending upon the nature of the transaction — and multiple debits or credits in each journal.

Exhibit J – Multi-column Journal

Cash Disbursements Journal
Period: May 19XX

Date	Payee	Check #	Cash (Cr)	Mchdse (Dr)	Advertising (Dr)	Utilities (Dr)	Equipment Rental (Dr)	Insurance (Dr)	Other	
									Acct #	Amount (Dr)
5/03	Acme Products	2434	327.50	327.50						
5/05	Smith Productions	2435	750.00		750.00					
5/06	Western Power	2436	145.00			145.00				
5/09	Bates Rentals	2437	77.00				77.00			
5/11	Kline Insurance	2438	750.00					750.00		
5/17	Void	2439	0.00							
5/22	World Bank	2440	38.00						Bk Chg	38.00
5/31	Acme Products	2441	975.00	975.00						
	Total for Month		3,062.50	1,302.50	750.00	145.00	77.00	750.00		38.00

Summary of Other Checks
Bank Charges   38.00

Exhibit J illustrates a cash disbursements journal. Since cash is being expended by the company, thereby reducing an asset, one column must be used to credit the Cash account — see Table 9, Chart of Accounts. Since only one column is used for the credit, all other columns are available for debits. The advantage of this will be realized when posting (transferring) individual transaction amounts from the journals to the multi-columned general ledger — it permits the accountant to head a column with any frequently occurring type of transaction.

In Exhibit J, Merchandise, Advertising, Utilities, Equipment Rental, and Insurance are used as column headings. This is because the hypothetical business has numerous transactions in each of these accounts.

The advantage of this type of journal is that, at the end of an accounting period, the accountant can add each column down; when all of the columns are totaled, the total sum of all debits should equal the sum of all credits. If they "balance" (are equal), the journal has been added correctly. If they do not balance, the accountant must find the error.

Notice that the heading at the top of the page identifies the specific type of journal. It should also show the time period being accounted for. The first (left-hand) column should show the date of the transaction, followed by a description of the transaction in the larger column to its right. Multicolumn journals differ from the two-column general journal in the description portion of the entry. The transaction account is shown as the description in the general journal, while in multicolumn journals, the description should be the name of the person or company receiving the check.

In Exhibit J, Kline Insurance was paid $750 on May 11. The next column should list the check number — all checks should be listed in numerical order. Even if a check is "voided" (destroyed), list it in the journal and under "Description," write "void." This will simplify the accountant's bank reconciliation and provide a better audit trail for outsiders.

The remaining columns should be used for all frequently occurring debit transactions. Again, observe the specific column headings used in the example. Although only a portion of the journal may be used, it can be assumed that each of the transactions listed as column headings is a frequently occurring transaction.

The last two columns should be reserved for infrequently occurring transactions. The first of these two columns should give a description identifying the transaction account related to that check. The second column should be used to enter the dollar amount of the transaction.

Summary of Journal Types

In the following summary, the two types of journals discussed above become easily distinguishable.

Two-column journals:

- Are always used as a general journal,
- Must have both a debit and a credit column, and
- Must have either a detailed schedule appended to the journal verifying the dollar amount of the transaction or an explanatory note under the transaction entry.

Multicolumn journals:

- Must have a heading identifying the journal,
- Must have either one debit or one credit column,
- Must include a debit and a credit entry in each transaction entry,
- Must identify the source of the transaction in the description column, and
- Must have one debit column and the rest credit columns, or the reverse — one credit column and the rest debit columns.

In all journals, the total dollar value of debits must always equal the total dollar value of credits.

The General Ledger

The general ledger is used to aggregate all activity in the individual account(s) after all transactions for a given accounting period have been entered into the appropriate journals.

The general ledger is a book or group of two-column pages which contain one page for each transaction account (cash, accounts receivable, sales, salary expense and other accounts). The following examples will illustrate the proper form and usage of the general ledger and how to transfer (post) transaction entries from the journals to the general ledger.

There are two advantages to the general ledger:

- It aggregates all transactions for a given transaction account in one place, thereby making it easier to analyze each transaction account; and
- It is easier to prepare your financial statements (balance sheet and income statement) since all transaction accounts are totaled.

Exhibits K-1, K-2, and K-3 are examples of the format of a general ledger page. Several more examples are included in Exhibit M. Remember, there must be one general ledger page for every transaction account in your chart of accounts.

Exhibit K-1 – General Ledger: Cash in Bank

General Ledger
Transaction Account: Cash in Bank
Account Number: 100

Date	Posting Reference	Debit	Credit
5/01	Beginning Balance	2,500.00	
5/31	Cash Disbursements Journal		3,062.50
5/31	Cash Receipts Journal	3,750.00	
5/31	General Journal		57.50
5/31	Ending Balance	3,130.00	
6/01	Beginning Balance	3,130.00	
6/30	Cash Disbursements Journal		4,000.00
6/30	Cash Receipts Journal	3,500.00	
6/30	Ending Balance	2,630.00	

The three examples shown are cash in bank, accounts payable, and rent expense. Cash is a balance sheet "asset" account, accounts payable is a balance sheet "liability" account, and rent expense is an income statement "expense." Even though each account is in a different section in your financial statements, the format for each account is exactly the same. Account numbers are shown in each example. Whether you use them in your own accounting system depends on your personal preference, and the complexity of your accounting system.

Observe the four main sections of the general ledger: date, posting reference, debit and credit.

- Date. Write the date for which the entries are being made; regardless of the date on which the accounting work was performed, the date shown should be the last day of the month in which the transaction occurred.

- Posting reference. The posting reference identifies the journal from which the entered dollar total was transferred (posted). In the examples, dollar amounts were posted from the cash disbursements journal, cash receipts journal, purchases journal, and general journal. Notice in the posting reference column, the phrases "beginning balance" and "ending balance" appear — both of these items are explained later.

- Debit. Remember, in double-entry accounting, all entries are either debits or credits. Since you are posting from a journal the sum of all individual transactions for a period, that transferred sum may be either a debit or credit. In the Cash in Bank example, the sum transferred from the cash disbursements journal was a credit and the sum transferred from the cash receipts journal was a debit — since receipt of cash increases an asset.

- Credit. This column must also appear. See Debit, above.

These four columns must always be used in a general journal. After all of the journals have been completely posted — every transaction sum written in the general ledger — total the activity in the general ledger. This is accomplished by subtracting all of the credits from all of the debits. In Exhibit K-1 – Cash in Bank, three journals were posted in the month of May: cash disbursements journal ($3,062.50 credit); cash receipts journal ($3,750 debit); and general journal ($57.50 credit).

Journal	Debits	Credits
Cash Disbursements		$3,062.50
Cash Receipts	$3,750.00	
General Journal		$ 57.50
Total for Month	$3,750.00	$3,120.00

The difference between debits and credits for the month of May is $630.00, with the difference being a debit. The debits are larger than the credits by $630.00, which means the net monthly activity for May was $630.

This difference is added to the beginning balance for the account. In the example, the account balance was $2,500.00 on May 1 — note the balance was a debit balance. Since the month began with a debit balance and the sum of all activity for the month of May was also a debit, add the $2,500.00 to the $630.00. This produces the ending balance (May 31) of $3,130.00, as shown in the Cash in Bank example (Exhibit K-1).

Another way of looking at this is to add the beginning balance debit of $2,500 (May 1) to the cash receipts journal debit of $3,750 (May 31) which equals $6,250; then subtract the credit from the cash disbursements journal and the general journal ($3,120 combined) to get an ending balance of $3,130, which is a debit.

Any account can have a debit or credit balance at any time; this will be determined by the individual transactions.

To further illustrate this point, continue to look at the Cash in Bank example. The example continues with June activity. We have already seen how the ending balance of $3,130 was derived. Note the ending balance of a month is the same thing as the beginning balance for the next month.

Observe that in June there are two debits: the beginning balance of $3,130 and the cash receipts journal of $3,500. Adding the debits ($6,630) and subtracting the credit ($4,000) leaves a debit balance of $2,630.

Note that the net activity for the month of June was a credit of $500. Debits in June were $3,500, and credits were $4,000, yielding a $500 credit for the month of June, whereas the net activity in the month of May was a debit of $630. There is nothing positive or negative about debits and credits, they offset each other. Subtract one from the other and enter the dollar difference in either the debit or credit column — whichever is larger.

That is the significance of the Cash in Bank (Exhibit K-1) example. In May, debit activity for the month was greater than credit activity; therefore, the beginning balance was debited $630. The net effect is that an additional debit increases a debit balance and an additional credit decreases a debit balance. Similarly, an additional credit increases a credit balance and an additional debit decreases a credit balance.

Two additional examples of a general ledger page detailing activity in the accounts payable and rent expense transaction accounts follow.

Exhibit K-2 – General Ledger: Accounts Payable

General Ledger
Transaction Account: Accounts Payable
Account Number: 200

Date	Posting Reference	Debit	Credit
5/01	Beginning Balance		1,000.00
5/31	Purchases Journal		1,500.00
5/31	Cash Disbursements Journal	750.00	
5/31	Ending Balance		1,750.00
6/01	Beginning Balance		1,750.00
6/30	Purchases Journal		2,500.00
6/30	Cash Disbursements Journal	2,750.00	
6/30	General Journal	250.00	
6/30	Ending Balance		1,250.00

Exhibit K-3 – General Ledger: Rent Expense

General Ledger
Transaction Account: Rent Expense
Account Number: 645

Date	Posting Reference	Debit	Credit
5/01	Beginning Balance	500.00	
5/31	Cash Disbursements Journal	100.00	
5/31	Ending Balance	600.00	
6/01	Beginning Balance	600.00	
6/30	Cash Disbursements Journal	100.00	
6/30	Ending Balance	700.00	

Another way of looking at this is to add the beginning balance debit of $2,500 (May 1) to the cash receipts journal debit of $3,750 (May 31) which equals $6,250; then subtract the credit from the cash disbursements journal and the general journal ($3,120 combined) to get an ending balance of $3,130, which is a debit.

Any account can have a debit or credit balance at any time; this will be determined by the individual transactions.

To further illustrate this point, continue to look at the Cash in Bank example. The example continues with June activity. We have already seen how the ending balance of $3,130 was derived. Note the ending balance of a month is the same thing as the beginning balance for the next month.

Observe that in June there are two debits: the beginning balance of $3,130 and the cash receipts journal of $3,500. Adding the debits ($6,630) and subtracting the credit ($4,000) leaves a debit balance of $2,630.

Note that the net activity for the month of June was a credit of $500. Debits in June were $3,500, and credits were $4,000, yielding a $500 credit for the month of June, whereas the net activity in the month of May was a debit of $630. There is nothing positive or negative about debits and credits, they offset each other. Subtract one from the other and enter the dollar difference in either the debit or credit column — whichever is larger.

That is the significance of the Cash in Bank (Exhibit K-1) example. In May, debit activity for the month was greater than credit activity; therefore, the beginning balance was debited $630. The net effect is that an additional debit increases a debit balance and an additional credit decreases a debit balance. Similarly, an additional credit increases a credit balance and an additional debit decreases a credit balance.

Two additional examples of a general ledger page detailing activity in the accounts payable and rent expense transaction accounts follow.

Exhibit L-1 – Cash Receipts Journal

Cash Receipts Journal
Period: May 19XX

Date	Description	Invoice Number	Cash (Dr)	Sales (Cr)	Acc Rec (Cr)	Other Account	Amount (Cr)
5/03	Daily Cash Sales	Register	475.00	475.00			
5/03	W. Churchill	366	175.00		175.00		
5/07	Daily Cash Sales	Register	525.00	525.00			
5/10	Acme Products	none	15.00			Mchdse	15.00
5/19	G. Washington	362	385.00		385.00		
5/24	Daily Cash Sales	Register	600.00	600.00			
5/31	Bank of Pacific	none	5,000.00			Bank Loan	5,000.00
	Monthly Totals		7,175.00	1,600.00	560.00	0.00	5,015.00

(✓)

Summary of Other Entries
Merchandise   15.00
Bank Loans   5,000.00
                                       5,015.00

Daily Cash Sales: Total receipts from cash register

W. Churchill: Specific customer pays on account (accounts receivable)

Acme Products: Supplier sent check back to you (discount or rebate), reducing the cost of merchandise

Bank of Pacific: Borrowed money from bank, a liability (loan payable or bank loan)

Notice that the debits ($7,175.00) equal the sum of the credit columns ($1,600.00 + $560.00 + $5,015.00). Always total each column and verify that the debits equal the credits — this procedure is also called footing.

In addition, notice that the Other Entries column is summarized below the column total. This is to facilitate posting each transaction to its appropriate general ledger account page.

Other points to note include:

- A single underline means that the column is going to be added (or summed).

- A double underline means that the above number is the column total, ending the month or period being accounted for. In addition, it signifies that any numbers below the double underline begin a new accounting period and any addition begins at "0".
- The check marks under the totals mean that the amounts have been posted to the general ledger. Exhibit L-1 – Cash Receipts Journal illustrates that the $7,175 has been posted to the general ledger. Do not make the check mark until you have physically posted to the general ledger.

Remember that all journals must be totaled in the same fashion — the underlining is important because it tells you what has been added, and the double underline indicates where the adding stops. The check marks are important because they tell what has been posted to the general ledger.

Cash Disbursements Journal

The cash disbursements journal, or CDJ (Exhibit L-2), is used whenever the business writes checks. Since cash, an asset, is being reduced, cash is a credit in this journal.

Every transaction includes an expenditure of cash, and the offsetting (equal) amount is distributed to the transaction account which is appropriate to the specific transaction (event).

Exhibit L-2 – Cash Disbursements Journal

Cash Disbursements Journal
Period: May 19XX

Date	Payee	Check #	Cash (Cr)	Mchdse (Dr)	Advertising (Dr)	Utilities (Dr)	Equipment Rental (Dr)	Insurance (Dr)	Other Acct #	Other Amount (Dr)
5/03	Acme Products	2434	327.50	327.50						
5/05	Smith Productions	2435	750.00		750.00					
5/06	Western Power	2436	145.00			145.00				
5/09	Bates Rentals	2437	77.00				77.00			
5/11	Kline Insurance	2438	750.00					750.00		
5/17	Void	2439	0.00							
5/22	World Bank	2440	38.00						Bk Chg	38.00
5/31	Acme Products	2441	975.00	975.00						
	Total for Month		3,062.50	1,302.50	750.00	145.00	77.00	750.00		38.00

Summary of Other Checks
Bank Charges   38.00

Individual entries in the cash disbursements journal include:

Acme Products: Paid supplier of merchandise for resale, increase of asset, therefore, debit merchandise inventory

Western Power: Paid electric company, increases an expense account, therefore debit utility expense

Once the columns have been added, they are double underlined and check marked, like those in the cash receipt journal.

Purchases Journal

The purchases journal, or PJ (Exhibit L-3), is used whenever products, services, or supplies are purchased on open account from your company's suppliers or vendors and are not immediately paid for.

Accounts payable is always the credit account in this journal. Since your company owes more money with each transaction and this increases a liability, you must credit each to accounts payable. Every transaction includes an increase in accounts payable and the equal amount is distributed to the appropriate transaction account.

The format for Merchandise Purchases shown in Exhibit L-3 can be varied. You may use only one column for all of your inventory or you may use multiple columns to track major inventory lines, as in this example. If you use multiple columns for your inventory control, you can also set up a general ledger account for each major line of your merchandise inventory or you can use one general account, as is done in Exhibit M.

Individual entries in the purchases journal include:

Furniture World: Equipment is being rented from this supplier, and they have invoiced you for the next month. An expense is increased. Debit Other: Equipment Rental.

Booty World: You have taken delivery of a shipment of shoes for resale. This increases an asset. Debit Merchandise Purchases.

Again, notice that the debits equal the credits. As with the other journals, the check marks indicate that the column totals have been posted to the appropriate general ledger accounts.

Exhibit L-3 – Purchases Journal

Purchase Journal
Period: May 19XX

Date	Description	Invoice #	Accounts Payable (Cr)	Merchandise Purchases			Other	
				Shoes (Dr)	Clothing (Dr)	Other (Dr)	Acct #	Amount (Dr)
5/06	Milner, Inc.	313565	225.00		225.00			
5/09	Booty World	223	175.00	175.00				
5/13	Ties Anonymous	7933	250.00			250.00		
5/17	Furniture World	22234	75.00				Equip Rent	75.00
5/24	Acme Products	997	175.00	175.00				
5/31	Milner, Inc.	B13578	200.00		200.00			
	Total for Month		1,100.00	350.00	425.00	250.00		75.00

Summary of Other Purchases
Equipment Rental   75.00

Exhibit M, following, includes all of the general ledger accounts affected by the journals in Exhibits L-1–3. Observe that the account balances (sum of the columns) in the journals have been posted exactly from the journals to the appropriate general ledger account.

Exhibit M – General Ledger Accounts

Cash in Bank
Account Number 100

Date	Posting Reference	Debit	Credit
5/01	Beginning Balance	1 200.00	
5/31	Cash Receipts Jrnl	7,175.00	
5/31	Cash Disbursements		3,062.50
5/31	Ending Balance	5,312.50	

Accounts Receivable
Account Number 110

Date	Posting Reference	Debit	Credit
5/01	Beginning Balance	6,200.00	
5/31	Cash Receipts Jrnl		560.00
5/31	Ending Balance	5,640.00	

Merchandise Inventory
Account Number 120

Date	Posting Reference	Debit	Credit
5/01	Beginning Balance	2,500.00	
5/31	Cash Disbursements	1,302.50	
5/31	Purchases Jrnl	1,025.00	
5/31	Cash Receipts Jrnl		15.00
5/31	Ending Balance	4,812.50	

Accounts Payable
Account Number 200

Date	Posting Reference	Debit	Credit
5/01	Beginning Balance		2,500.00
5/31	Purchases Jrnl		1,100.00
5/31	Ending Balance		3,600.00

Bank Loan
Account Number 260

Date	Posting Reference	Debit	Credit
5/01	Beginning Balance		0.00
5/31	Cash Receipts Jrnl		5,000.00
5/31	Ending Balance		5,000.00

Owners Capital
Account Number 300

Date	Posting Reference	Debit	Credit
5/01	Beginning Balance		14,500.00
5/31	Ending Balance		1,450.00

Sales
Account Number 400

Date	Posting Reference	Debit	Credit
5/01	Beginning Balance		15,000.00
5/31	Cash Receipts Jrnl		1,600.00
5/31	Ending Balance		16,600.00

Advertising
Account Number 600

Date	Posting Reference	Debit	Credit
5/01	Beginning Balance	3,000.00	
5/31	Cash Disbursements	750.00	
5/31	Ending Balance	3,750.00	

Exhibit M – General Ledger Accounts (continued)

Insurance Expense
Account Number 610

Date	Posting Reference	Debit	Credit
5/01	Beginning Balance	4,500.00	
5/31	Cash Disbursements	750.00	
5/31	Ending Balance	5,250.00	

Equipment Rental
Account Number 627

Date	Posting Reference	Debit	Credit
5/01	Beginning Balance	525.00	
5/31	Cash Disbursements	77.00	
5/31	Purchases Jrnl	75.00	
5/31	Ending Balance	677.00	

Utilities
Account Number 655

Date	Posting Reference	Debit	Credit
5/01	Beginning Balance	900.00	
5/31	Cash Disbursements	145.00	
5/31	Ending Balance	1,045.00	

Bank Charges
Account Number 675

Date	Posting Reference	Debit	Credit
5/01	Beginning Balance	125.00	
5/31	Cash Disbursements	38.00	
5/31	Ending Balance	163.00	

There is one general ledger account (page) for every transaction account appearing in all of the journals. Remember, there must be a general ledger page for each transaction account being used in your accounting system. Just because there is an account for a specific transaction does not mean it will be used every month — sometimes there will be no entries for a given account for varying time periods.

Look at the first account of the General Ledger Accounts, Cash in Bank. The beginning balance as of May 1 was $1,200. This means that as of that date you had $1,200 in the bank. The next two entries represent the cash transactions which occurred during the month of May. The $7,175 from the cash receipts journal was posted to the general ledger — the same amount as is shown in the Cash Receipts Journal. You also posted $3,062.50 from the Cash Disbursements Journal to the General Ledger — the same amount as is shown in the Cash Disbursements Journal.

In a similar way, look at every entry in every general ledger account — Merchandise Inventory, Advertising, Sales, Accounts

Payable. Note in the table below, the source of every entry in the general ledger is a column in one of the journals.

General Ledger Account	Amount	Journal Source
Accounts Receivable	$ 560.00 (credit)	Cash Receipts Journal
Merchandise Inventory	$1,025.00 (debit)	Purchases Journal
Sales	$1,600.00 (credit)	Cash Receipts Journal
Advertising Expense	$ 750.00 (debit)	Cash Disbursements Journal
Rental Expense	$ 75.00 (debit)	Purchases Journal

By comparing each general ledger entry to each of the journal examples, you can verify that every column in every journal has been posted to its appropriate transaction account in the general ledger pages.

Once you have posted all of the transactions from the journals to the general ledger, you are ready to prepare the periodic financial statements — the Income Statement and the Balance Sheet which are shown in Appendix I. The examples are based on a running balance in the general ledger — the totals shown in the general ledger at any time of the year reflect the sum of all of the business activity for the entire year-to-date. The totals shown in the journal examples, also reflect all activity from January 1, 19xx through May 31, 19xx.

Closing the General Ledger

Preparing the financial statements is known as closing the books. The first step in the closing procedure is to total the individual general ledger transaction accounts. This is the process of offsetting the debits and credits in each transaction account.

For instance, from the Cash in Bank account, you take the beginning balance debit ($1,200.00), add the May transaction debit ($7,175), and subtracted the May transaction credit ($3,062.50). This is how you calculate the May 31 ending balance ($5,312.50).

The ending balance takes a debit because the total of the debits was greater than the total of the credits. If the reverse were true, the total would be shown in the credit column. Look at the Accounts Payable transaction account in the Exhibit M – General Ledger Accounts examples. You can see it had a beginning credit balance and the only transaction activity for the month of May was also a credit balance. In this case, add the beginning balance credit to the May activity credit. The total equals the ending balance.

Preparing the Financial Statements

Once you have totaled all of the general ledger accounts, it is time to prepare the financial statements. Remember, in totaling each account, there are no pluses or minuses, only debits and credits. Add all of the debits, then total all of the credits. The difference between the two amounts is your ending balance — a debit if the debits were larger or a credit if the credits were larger.

The Working Trial Balance, shown next, is simply a listing of all of the accounts in the general ledger with each account's ending balance. The example, illustrates the working trial balance. The source of the accounts and balances in this example is the General Ledger Accounts example, Exhibit M. Each general ledger account in that example is written on the working trial balance. Also observe that the ending balance for each account is written in the first two columns.

The key components of the working trial balance are:

- A column for account names
- Two columns for ending balance
- Two columns for income statement
- Two columns for balance sheet

If you are using transaction account numbers, use the small column on the left to show the number. Two columns are used for the balances to show the debit and the credit in separate columns.

Exhibit N – Working Trial Balance

ABC Company
Working Trial Balance
May 31, 19XX

Account	Balance (Dr)	Balance (Cr)	Income Statement (Dr)	Income Statement (Cr)	Balance Sheet (Dr)	Balance Sheet (Cr)
Cash In Bank	5,312.50				5,312.50	
Accounts Receivable	5,640.00				5,640.00	
Merchandise Inventory	4,812.50				4,812.50	
Accounts Payable		3,600.00				3,600.00
Bank Loan		5,000.00				5,000.00
Owners Capital		1,450.00				1,450.00
Sales		16,600.00		16,600.00		
Advertising Expense	3,750.00		3,750.00			
Insurance Expense	5,250.00		5,250.00			
Equipment Rental	677.00		677.00			
Utilities Expense	1,045.00		1,045.00			
Bank Charges	163.00		163.00			
Profit from Income Statement						5,715.00
Total for Month	26,650.00	26,650.00	10,885.00	16,600.00	15,765.00	15,765.00

In the Working Trial Balance example, the ending balance columns are exactly equal. Debits must equal credits! Once you have posted the ending balances from the general ledger to the first two columns of the working trial balance, total the debits and credits. If they are equal, there are no errors. If they are not equal, you must find the mistake. Remember, you have already verified that there were no mistakes in the journals by adding all debits and credits in each journal and verifying that they are equal. Therefore, you probably posted a balance incorrectly from the general ledger. Three steps can be taken to find an error at this point, assuming there is one.

- Look for an account balance that is the same as the discrepancy. It is not uncommon to miss an account when you initially post the trial balance.

- Divide the difference by two, then look for the result in your general ledger. A number has likely been posted as a debit when it is a credit, or vice versa.

- Divide the difference by nine. If the result is a whole number — not a fraction — there is a transposition error, which probably occurred while posting from the general ledger.

If a mistake was made, one of the above three steps should discover it.

Finally, if the difference is minor, it is quite permissible to make the books balance by including the difference as a sundry expense item. We recommend that you perform the above three steps first to ensure that you don't have two large offsetting errors. Once you have verified that this is not the case, to write off differences of one or two dollars is much better use of your time than looking for such a trivial difference.

If, after posting the ending balances on the working trial balance, the debit column exactly equals the credit column, your work is essentially over.

As you can see from the example, only two more steps are required:

- Transfer the ending balance for all balance sheet accounts (both debit and credit) across the page to the balance sheet columns.
- Transfer the ending balance for all income statement accounts (both debit and credit) across the page to the income statement columns.

You have now prepared both the balance sheet and the income statement. Observe in the income statement that the debit column does not equal the credit column. This is because the company either made a profit or sustained a loss. If the credits are larger than the debits on the income statement, your company made a profit. If the debits are larger, your company had a loss. When your sales are larger than your expenses, your company is profitable. When your expenses are larger than your sales, you have suffered a loss.

In the income statement portion of the Working Trial Balance example, the total sales exceed the sum of all the expenses. This means the business made a profit of $5,175.00. Had the expenses exceeded the sales, the business would have suffered a loss.

You have now completed the accounting cycle! You may want to transfer the balance sheet and income statement numbers to a different format. See Chapter 2, What Is A Financial Statement?, for different statement formats.

If the period accounted for does not require any external reporting — IRS, bank, or bonding company — you need do nothing further. You can clearly see the results of the business on the trial balance. However, if you need to show the results to somebody outside the business, choose an appropriate statement format and transfer the numbers to that format.

The basic accounting cycle is completed. It is really quite simple — it only requires time and inclination on your part. A final recommendation: you should retain the services of a qualified accountant to assist you at first. Your tax preparer or a small accounting firm are logical places to look. A small investment in professional services at the outset can save a considerable sum of money later on — both in dollars you do not have to spend for basic accounting work and the possible cost of having to hire an accountant to clean up an error-laden mess.

Payroll Schedules

You have already seen how the accounting cycle works. There are several other functions you may need to understand to perform the accounting function yourself. These include payroll, depreciation, and bank reconciliations. This section will illustrate a basic approach to performing your own payroll services.

If you have numerous employees, you may want to retain a payroll service. Your local bank or other independent service — Automatic Data Processing (ADP), for example — can provide payroll assistance, for a fee. However, if you have relatively few employees, you may want to perform the payroll work yourself.

The Exhibit O – Payroll Register example illustrates a workable payroll format. It is based on 1997 California tax rates. You may have different taxes depending on the state or city in which you reside. You can verify your responsibilities by contacting your local tax authorities or retaining a qualified professional to assist you in the beginning. In addition to federal and state parole tax information, you will also want to find out if you have any local payroll taxes.

Exhibit O – Payroll Register

ABC Semiconductor, Inc.
Payroll Register
Period Ending June 15, 19XX

| Name | Gross Salary | Federal | | | State | | Net Salary |
		W/H	FICA	Medicare	W/H	SDI	
Joe Smith	$3,000.00	$320.90	$186.00	$ 43.50	$145.00	$27.00	$2,278.50
Eve White	2,250.00	407.00	139.50	32.63	133.60	20.25	1,517.02
Chris Jones	1,875.00	190.00	116.25	37.19	51.50	16.88	1,473.18
Company Total	$7,125.00	$917.90	$441.75	$103.32	$330.10	$64.13	$5,267.80

In the example, the column headings are restricted to Employee Name, Gross Salary, and several payroll deductions. In the state of California, these include State Withholding and a State Disability Tax. In all states, the federal withholding will be the same. Following are the sources for withholding information.

Federal Withholding

This is the employee's income tax obligation to the federal government. You can obtain a federal personal income tax guide from your local Internal Revenue Service office. The guide contains tax withholding tables for married and single people that show you the proper withholding amount for each individual.

Social Security (FICA)

This is a federal retirement insurance assessed on all for-profit employers. This is a stated percentage (7.65% in 1997) which should be deducted from each employee's pay. The 7.65% assessment includes 6.20% for federal retirement insurance and 1.45% for medicare.

State Withholding

Employee's income tax obligation to the state. You can request a state income tax guide from your local state tax authority. It will contain tables similar to the federal guide.

State Disability Insurance (SDI) – a California tax

Your state tax authority may not have this tax, but it may have something similar. The state tax authority will inform you of any such obligations. In California, this tax is a percentage of gross income — similar to FICA.

A payroll register performs three functions:

- It calculates each employee's net pay,
- It acts as accounting source documentation for your accounting system, and
- It provides source information for federal and state tax forms.

When you use this format, remember to add all of the columns, and verify that the gross salary column equals the sum of all other columns. This check will discover any arithmetic errors.

Additionally, this form is a source of information for your employer tax responsibilities. There are certain employer taxes as well as employee taxes. It is advisable to either telephone each tax authority and verify your individual obligations or consult a qualified professional accountant to assist you in the beginning. The tax authorities can be quite helpful in assisting you. You do not want to make mistakes with tax authorities — they frequently penalize you for underpayments.

Depreciation

In your accounting system there are certain nonpaper transactions you have to remember to enter in your general journal. Depreciation is one of these. You should establish a cost level — for example, $500.00 — under which any purchase of tools or machines is expensed in the current period and entered in an account called, for example, Small Tools Expense.

If the amount of the purchase is greater than $500.00, and the purchased equipment has a useful life in excess of one year, you can not write off the entire cost in the current period. This is what is called a fixed asset — machinery, building, and leasehold improvements. These items must be entered into the accounting system as an asset.

The way you recognize the cost of such an asset is by depreciation. If you purchased a computer for $5,000.00, you enter a fixed asset in your accounting system and recognize the cost of the asset on a monthly basis over the life of that asset. In the computer example, let us assume that it will be usable for a period of five years. Therefore, a certain percentage of that cost will be expensed in your general ledger on a monthly basis for five years.

There are different methods of depreciation. The most conservative method is called straight line depreciation. This means dividing the cost of the asset by the number of months the asset is useful.

In the computer example, we assumed a five-year (60-month) useful life.

Thus:

$$\frac{\$5,000}{60 \text{ months}} = \$83.33$$

Each month you should expense $83.33 for depreciation of the computer. Each asset is treated the same way. Since most businesses have more than one asset, you should have a schedule that lists all of your depreciable assets. The next schedule illustrated is called a schedule of fixed assets.

Exhibit P – Schedule of Fixed Assets

ABC Semiconductor, Inc.
Schedule of Fixed Assets

Asset Number	Description	Purchase Date	Serial Number	Cost	Useful Life	Monthly Depreciation
1	Furnace	2/23/XX	SCF101	$ 7,500.00	7 Years	$ 89.29
2	Furnace	2/23/XX	SCF106	7,500.00	7 Years	89.29
3	Spinner	2/28/XX	101193	4,500.00	5 Years	75.00
4	Implanter	3/31/XX	546XD33	95,000.00	7 Years	1,130.95
5	Clean Room	4/02/XX	None	75,000.00	10 Years	625.00
Total				$189,500.00		$2,009.53

The schedule of fixed assets should contain sufficient information to easily identify each asset. As you can see in the example, there is certain information to identify the asset and certain information to calculate the monthly depreciation of that asset. If you want to update the schedule on a regular basis, you can add a column called Accumulated Depreciation. This would simply update the total depreciation recognized up to the date of the schedule. If this is too much work, you can simply update the schedule whenever additional fixed assets are purchased.

Again, you may need qualified assistance to determine which depreciation methods are legal and which methods provide you with the best tax advantages.

Bank Reconciliation

Cash is King! This is an important cliché in business — believe it! Always know your cash balance. It is easily effected by preparing a monthly bank reconciliation. A bank reconciliation is performed by taking your bank statement, making certain adjustments to that balance, and comparing the adjusted total to the cash balance in your balance sheet. If your bank does not end your statement period on the last day of the month you could talk to your bank manager and request a change of your reporting period, so your bank statement period will end on the last day of the calendar month.

The next example illustrates a bank reconciliation. Descriptions of the specific line examples follow.

Balance per bank statement

This is the ending balance shown on the front of your monthly bank statement.

Add

Any increases to your cash account that you have recognized in your accounting system that the bank statement does not reflect. They are as follows:

- Deposit in Transfer. These are bank deposits you made in your accounting system that the bank may not have entered in your account until the next month — one or two days later.

- Bank Error. Always compare your canceled checks to the amount shown on the bank statement — banks do occasionally make errors. If there is an error, promptly contact your bank.

Deduct

Any decreases to your cash account recognized in your accounting system that the bank statement does not reflect. Deductions include outstanding checks. These are checks which have been written but have not cleared your bank as of the end of the accounting period. You have already recognized these in your cash disbursements journal. Your balance sheet has the right cash balance, so you have to deduct these amounts from the bank statement.

Adjusted bank balance

This is the sum of the Balance Per Bank Statement plus Total Add, less Total Deduct.

Balance per books

This is the amount shown in the balance sheet. The balance per book must equal the adjusted bank balance. If they are not equal, you must find the difference.

Exhibit Q – Bank Reconciliation

ABC Semiconductor, Inc.
Bank Reconciliation

Balance Per Bank Statement:		$12,333.98
Add:		
Deposit in Transit	$3,500.00	
Bank Error (Check #9877)	25.00	
Total Add		3,525.00
Deduct:		
Outstanding Checks:		
#9902	1,255.00	
#9903	25.57	
#9904	112.34	
#9905	986.75	
#9906	644.45	
Total Deduct		(3,024.11)
Adjusted Bank Balance		$12,834.87
Balance Per Books		$12,834.87
In Reconciliation ✓		

All of the transactions recognized in your accounting system must be recognized in your adjusted bank balance. If there is an error, look for items which appear in one place, but not the other, such as:

- Bank charges on the bank statement not in your accounting system;
- Wire transfers or other non-check disbursements or receipts which are in the bank statement, but not in your books; and

- Temporary checks — if you ran out of regular checks — which are in the bank statement but not in your books.

Do not close your books (end the monthly accounting cycle) without first performing a bank reconciliation — if an error in cash was made, the reconciliation will find it. If there is an error, you will want to make a general journal entry to correct the error.

Times to Consult an Accountant

As you have seen, the basic concepts and activities of accounting are fairly simple. Some aspects of accounting, though can become quite complex and you would be wise to obtain qualified assistance with them.

If you choose to perform your own accounting, the expenditure of a few dollars at the outset, to make sure you are on the right track, can be a wise investment. Then, you should be able to comfortably perform your own accounting function, although you will probably still want assistance filling out various tax forms.

Should you choose not to perform your own accounting function, the preceding information will still enable you to better understand your business. Always remember, accounting is a score-keeping function. It can tell you much about the operation of your business. The more you know about your business, the better you are able to run that business!

Chapter 5

Automated Bookkeeping

Accounting Systems

The usefulness of an accounting system is derived from a blend of the quality and timeliness of information yielded, and the ease with which the data is maintained and processed. The simpler a system is to use, the better it will be maintained, and the faster and more accurate the information it will produce.

The biggest problem with accounting is the duplication of effort required to manually maintain your financial records. Bookkeeping is a matter of balance and symmetry. Each transaction has an effect and a corresponding opposite effect, thus the term double-entry bookkeeping. Double-entry bookkeeping requires a minimum of two entries for every transaction. As the volume of your business increases, so does the number of transactions that require processing by your accounting system. As this happens it becomes exceedingly important to reduce the duplication of work effort.

Automated systems work on the basis you need only process each item once. The system then automatically processes the other side of the transaction. An automated system is one that reduces the duplication of effort in recording your financial affairs. These range from the utilitarian one-write system to complex computer software. All require some set up and all require entries to be made, but from there on they provide utility. The system that is best for you and your business is the one that both reduces your recordkeeping time and improves the timing and quality of your financial data and reports.

The One-write System

Automating your accounting system is one solution to the problem of excess duplication. This does not mean that you need to immediately buy a computer and sophisticated software packages; rather, the first step is to consider a one-write system. One-write systems are manually maintained, but are designed to reduce the duplication of effort by recording transactions through the simple use of carbon copy material.

In reality, most businesses maintain the initial recording of financial transactions on paper. For instance, when an order is received from a customer by phone — you listen and you write. Only later does this transaction get entered into the accounting system. Similarly, when you write a check, it isn't until later that you enter it into the register as the source of input to record the payment in the accounting records. By analyzing the steps that are taken in this example of writing a check you will see where the duplication of effort occurs and where it can be avoided. The steps are:

become up-to-date transaction records and summaries with a one-write system. As described below, the other routines of recording your business transactions also lend themselves to a one-write system and can significantly reduce the effort necessary in maintaining accounting records.

Payroll

The routines required in the preparation of a payroll can also be simplified by using a one-write system. When you prepare the payroll, all withholding and gross pay information can be copied onto each employee's pay record through the carbon on the payroll summary. This procedure is done at the same time that the employee's check is prepared. A very time-consuming process has been simplified by avoiding the need to recopy the information, and the employee's pay record card is always up-to-date.

Sales

The sales cycle lends itself best to using a one-write system as a cash receipts log that copies the receipt onto each customer card. However, while it is possible to use this approach to record customer invoices onto their cards, it could be cumbersome, especially when customer invoices are to be typed — it can be done, but is not particularly effective as a time and effort saver.

Payables

In an accrual system, it is necessary to record amounts owed to suppliers as payables when their invoices are received — not just when you pay them. The greater the number of suppliers, the more difficult it is to determine how much each is owed. In addition, banks often charge for each check written. Therefore, it is more cost efficient to write checks to suppliers at regular, less-frequent intervals, paying for more than one invoice per check.

The most common way to record this activity is to maintain a separate card for each supplier, showing the activity with that supplier and the current amount owed. To facilitate this, an accounts payable journal is maintained with each invoice being recorded as it is received. When this journal is coded and totaled it becomes the payables journal, recording the expense side of each invoice and the total of payables incurred.

As each invoice is recorded, the supplier or vendor card is positioned beneath and each transaction is copied through the carbon to maintain and update the card. The payment to each supplier is recorded by placing the supplier's card between the check and the cash disbursements journal when the check is written. The only other action required in updating the supplier's card is to record the new balance on the card.

Inventory

Manufacturing and wholesale businesses can find a one-write system to be a cost-efficient method of recording both physical quantities and prices of parts and raw materials. The method of using a one-write system is similar to that of payables but the source documents are usually

- suppliers' invoices for parts received and
- customer invoices for inventory shipped out.

As your business becomes more complex and other areas evolve which require double recording of transactions, the one-write system can be used to reduce duplication. In this process you will be dealing with the interaction of documents designed to control the flow of your business and to protect your assets. Accounting controls and the effects on and benefits to your business are dealt with later in this section, but they often tend to create additional paperwork. The sensible use of a one-write system in conjunction with these control documents can reduce duplication while providing up-to-date information.

Once you have moved into a one-write system, step back and observe the effect the system has had on your accounting records. Your accounting system has evolved. It is now more formalized and has set routines. The journals which were merely a method of summarizing and posting your transactions are now control documents that assist you in balancing the books.

The one-write approach has also changed where detailed information is contained and summarized. For instance, if information is needed about a supplier, all details of business dealings with that supplier are documented on the supplier's card; the total amounts owed are contained in the general ledger.

You have painlessly moved from a simple form of bookkeeping to a sophisticated set of accounting records with modules for each type of transaction. A one-write system may seem cumbersome at first, since it requires correct positioning of the forms prior to recording the transaction. However, the combination of time saved, error avoidance, and additional detail more than compensates for the initial effort in getting used to how each piece is properly placed.

The "evolutionary" effect of the one-write system on journals and books and how each part interrelates to produce your financial statements and other data is described below.

Checks

Writing checks also results in the creation of a cash disbursements journal, which gives a total without recording each transaction twice in the cash records. The detailed transactions are coded and summarized on the same ledger page and again posted by total only.

Payables invoices

These are recorded simultaneously on a payables journal and the suppliers' cards. The payables journal is then totaled and posted in summary. Checks made out to suppliers are also copied onto the suppliers' cards at the same time they are copied onto the cash disbursements journal. Each supplier card lets you know at a glance how much you owe to that supplier.

Payroll checks

Payroll amounts are copied onto the individual employee records and the payroll journal when the checks are written. The totals are then posted in summary only. Many small businesses dispense with the payroll journal and record payroll transactions directly onto the cash disbursements journal. This is perfectly acceptable, but may become inefficient when the number of employees exceeds ten or twelve.

Sales invoices

The sales invoice journal, customer card, and customer statement are all prepared simultaneously through one-write copies. The sales journal is then posted in summary only.

Cash receipts

The cash receipts journal, customer card, and customer statement are recorded simultaneously. The cash receipts journal is then posted in summary only.

The Computer and Bookkeeping

There was a time when computerizing an accounting system meant employing vast numbers of people and installing complex, expensive accounting machines or computers in huge air-conditioned rooms. Now the computer is in the price range of every business. It is compact and relatively simple to use. Modern computer accounting packages continue the principle of the one-write system, but with the added advantage that they also summarize and post your entries. Modern accounting software consists of a powerful data base with user friendly input screens and pre-prepared reports.

The computer has revolutionized the bookkeeping process. Gone are the days of endless columns of figures that never seem to balance — they have been replaced by printouts that boast internal accuracy. Unfortunately, the precision of the computer-generated statement is misleading. The computer has no inter-pretative soul — if you enter garbage, the computer will process and print garbage, but so neatly that you may be tempted to believe it is correct. This section is designed to give you a basic understanding of computerized bookkeeping that will help make the computer work for you, producing meaningful and reliable financial information. Used properly, the computer will reduce many of the repetitive tasks, but it will not reduce the amount of thought you need to exercise.

Important areas to consider before buying computer hardware and accounting software packages are discussed first.

Hardware

The term hardware refers to the computer and peripheral equipment (monitor, printer, and other add ons).

Central Processing Unit (CPU)

The "brains" of the computer system consists of a central processing unit (CPU) which processes electrical signals created by typing on the keyboard, and by the software installed in the machine (see "Software," page 111). In addition, the computer also contains one or more disk or tape drives, which are used to extract and store data. The computer uses internal memory, called random access memory (RAM), to process data.

Storage disks or tapes

These are media for storing data electronically, and they work in a manner similar to an audio compact disc or tape. There are two types of disk storage — floppy and hard disks. A floppy disk is portable, inexpensive, comes in two basic sizes (3 1/2 inch and, less usually, 5 1/4 inch), and has limited storage capacity. A hard disk, often permanently installed in the computer, offers faster access to data and can have considerable storage capacity. Tapes are inexpensive and tend to have limited storage capacity, but provide a simple alternative for backing up data. Other alternatives for backup are zip drives and removable hard drives.

Monitor

This is the visual display, much like a television screen. Most monitors are now color, but can be monochrome, meaning that they use a single color, usually either amber, gray, or green. Monitors offer different qualities of viewing due to the combination of the resolution capabilities of the monitor and the graphic capabilities of the computer. This is determined primarily by the video board and video memory installed — a special circuit board installed in the computer enabling it to render the correct visual display on the screen. As software has become more graphic, the quality and memory size of the video board has become much more important.

Printer

Printers are devices that work like electronic typewriters and enable you to print reports, graphs, and charts from the information processed by the computer. There are several types of printers available; price tends to be in direct proportion to the quality and speed of the printed output. The most common types of printers are dot matrix, ink jet, and laser printers. Of these, laser printers tend to be both faster and render better print quality than ink jet printers, but ink jet printers are considerably cheaper and many can also print in color. Dot matrix printers are most useful where you want to print on multipart forms. For instance, invoices where copies are required for shipping and accounts receivable as well as for the customer.

Computers and peripherals must fit your needs and be able to support your business as it grows. Despite the temptation, it is unlikely that you need state-of-the-art equipment. It is much more important that you buy reliable equipment which can be readily serviced and updated. Another factor in your choice of computer systems is that alternative equipment should be easy to come by if you should be without your computer for any length of time. There are currently two predominant types of systems: PCs or Personal Computers (sometimes called IBM or IBM compatible), and Apple computers.*

There are many decisions involved in selecting a particular machine. One consideration is price, but this should not be an overriding determinant. A second consideration is the comfort you feel in operating the computer; if it is difficult to operate, you will likely not get the best results from it. The third, and probably most important, is the software which is available for each machine. There is no easy way to say which machine is best suited for each business, situation, or user. However, you can learn a lot by finding out what equipment other people in your type of business are using and how comfortable they are with it. Another important step is to ask many questions of the salesperson before deciding which computer to buy.

Having said that, since most computers are purchased mail-order or from stores where the salesman knows little about the machines and nothing about accounting software, here are our suggestions of the important items to consider when buying hardware.

---

* IBM is a Registered Trademark of IBM Corporation. Apple is a Registered Trademark of Apple Computer, Inc.

- Software. First and foremost, decide which software you are going to use. Then read the system requirements written on the outside of the software package. This tells you minimum hardware requirements the software needs to run. It should address CPU, RAM, operating system, monitor, printer, input devices (mouse, keyboard, etc.), hard drive size, video memory and any other item of hardware configuration that is important.

- Memory. The computer should have sufficient memory capacity. In our experience, minimum memory configurations are just that. Satisfactory performance requires more RAM and video memory. When we first wrote this book we wrote "memory should be at least 640K, but preferably 1MB or more." Clearly more is true. Now a minimum configuration of 32MB is barely functional. As computers and software have improved, the graphic content and quality has grown exponentially.

- Storage. A hard disk drive is much faster and more useful than floppy disk drives alone, but you will require at least one floppy disk drive. A minimum of 2GB of hard drive space is essential, but 6GB is now common. In addition, a reliable back-up drive should be used. This can be inexpensively done by using a tape back-up drive.

- Printer. If you are using multi-part forms or checks a good 24 pin dot matrix printer is essential. However, if your printing is less extensive we recommend using a laser or ink-jet printer because it has more all round day to day functionality. Remember, that if you use an ink jet or laser printer that you should have your checks printed on single sheets for ease of use.

- CPU. Blinding operating speed is only necessary for the most complex calculations or for systems designed to be used by several people at once. A 133 mhz system will process most business applications, particularly accounting transactions, just as well as a 500 mhz system will.

- Monitor. A high resolution monitor is easier on the eyes than a lower quality or less expensive model. The reduced cost of high resolution color monitors makes them a reasonably priced alternative. Most software is now written for color monitors, so we recommend that you use one to get the most out of your system and software and to go easy on your eyes.

- Protective devices. A surge protector helps prevent loss of data due to sudden changes in electrical current. They are inexpensive and absolutely essential. Without one, a slight power surge, or spike, can destroy all the data loaded into the computer at that time.

- Cost consideration. The machine you select is likely to cost more than you want to pay, but less than you can afford. Remember, you can always upgrade or add to your system as you find it necessary and can afford it.

Software

Software consists of "intelligent" programs which translate typed commands and information into signals the computer can process. There are two basic types of software you will have in use on the computer at any one time.

Operating system

This is the set of operating instructions that translates the instructions typed into the computer and those instructions generated by your accounting program into signals the CPU can understand and process. The most common operating system used on PCs is Windows.*

Applications program

This is the subject-specific program that handles specified types of instructions. In this case, it would be the accounting program that will automate your accounting system. Another common example is a word processing package, which is used to type letters, memos, and reports. The primary problem with selecting software is the vast variety available. Options in selecting an operating system are generally limited, since most computers use only one specific type. Unfortunately, this is not the case with application programs, where there are many similar alternatives and all promise to be the best thing since sliced bread.

---

* Windows is a Registered Trademark of Microsoft Corporation.

Differentiating between programs and determining which one is best for you takes time and patience. A good place to start is with one of the surveys published by a computer magazine that covers the type of computer you are considering buying. This type of guide will help you in your decision, but it is essential that you analyze your business to determine what you need, rather than merely accepting what each program offers. Most small business owners and managers find that simple, inexpensive accounting software fulfills most of their needs in a format that is easy to work with. More elaborate and expensive packages usually deliver considerably more than is required, and are often more difficult to use. Your software package should have several features, including those discussed below.

Ease of processing

The format of the screen view should be easily recognizable and the flow of input for usual transaction tasks familiar. The more the system mimics how the paper would flow in a manual system, the easier it will be to use efficiently and effectively.

Out-of-balance edits

These are controls built into the accounting program which prevent the posting of transactions where the debits and credits are out of balance (do not equal each other) until the discrepancy has been corrected.

Audit trail

An audit trail consists of cross-referencing all processed transactions so that they can be readily identified and checked against the underlying documents.

Reports

Most current systems offer a wide range of built in reports — everything from budget and financial reports to sales by customer analysis — that can be produced at the click of a mouse button.

Protection from changing entered transactions

This feature prevents transactions from being changed once they have been processed except by a conscious override by the inputter.

Flexible chart of accounts

This is a chart of accounts which can be easily modified to suit the requirements of your business.

Integrated modules for payables, receivables, and payroll. Integrated modules are similar to the separate one-write systems for accounts receivable and payable, and payroll, discussed earlier. Transactions are entered in a separate subsystem — for instance, the accounts receivable module — the computer then processes the transactions, both within the subsystem and in the general ledger. There is no need to input any additional instructions or transactions.

Your software package should have either integrated modules for accounts payable, accounts receivable, and payroll; or additional modules for these which can be integrated into the system.

Security of access

Most security systems are designed to restrict access to your accounting system by requiring a password and/or access code to be entered first. Only the people you authorize can access it.

Overall ease of use

Any system will be of greater benefit if it is easy to work with and comfortable to use.

Other Considerations

If your business involves a significant amount of inventory, you should also consider an inventory module. This need not be expensive — we have used several simple accounting packages, and for most small businesses, the one we most often use has these integrated modules and retails for less than $150.

Identify Your Objectives

In order to obtain satisfactory results from a computerized system, it is necessary to visualize what you want the system to do. For most people, this means maintaining the same documents used when processing transactions by hand. The computer accounting package works similarly to a one-write system, but with a number of important differences.

Again, the most common example is seen in writing a check. When using a one-write system, a check is written, the carbon copies the detail onto the cash disbursements journal, and the journal is coded, totaled, and posted by hand. The trial balance and financial statements are then extracted.

With a computerized system, you write the check, code it, and input the detail into the computer. The computer then totals, posts, and prepares the trial balance and financial statements. Little time is saved in writing the check, but, with many transactions, the time saved by the computer for totaling and posting can be significant.

The detail available at the time of processing transactions, as well as accurate coding and input, is essential for accurate financial statements, just as they are in any manual accounting system.

Most small business owners find that by establishing regular accounting processing routines, they are able to maintain their accounting records in the most accurate and least time-consuming manner. This is usually done by regularly processing all transactions in the same order. It is often helpful to maintain a checklist to remind you of the routine and to check off as each is completed. Following is an example of such a checklist with the regular posting cycles.

Table 12 – Checklist for Routine Transaction Processing

Time Period	Routine Transactions and Tasks
Weekly	Cash disbursements
	Purchases
	Sales
	Cash receipts
	Payroll
	Print reports
	Back up all data
Monthly	Regular entries (depreciation, payroll taxes, etc.)
	Trial balance
	Adjusting journal entries (for correcting mistakes)
	Print general ledger, journal entries, financial statements for the month
	Close month
	Back up all data
Quarterly	Print quarterly payroll reports
	Print quarterly sales and sales tax reports
Annually	Final year-end adjustments
	Print special reports (such as payroll)
	Print all subledger detail (such as accounts payable and receivable)
	Print year-end general ledger, journal entries, and financial statements
	Close year off and start new year
	Back up all data

Two of these routines, which may not be familiar to you, deserve further explanation.

Backing up data

This is the process where data is copied to removable diskettes or tape. The procedure is usually described in detail in the software manual. Backing up data is important because it enables you to recreate all the postings that you have made with a minimum of effort, in the event that a problem with the system causes the data to be damaged or lost.

Closing the year

This is the process of finalizing the entries for the business' fiscal year and preparing to record transactions for the new year. This is usually done some time after the end of the year and not actually on the last day of the year. Since the value of all the balance sheet accounts is the same at the end of the old year as it is at the start of the new year, the accounts remain unchanged. However, the value of all the income statement accounts is zero at the start of the first day of the new year.

The process of closing the old year consists of bringing all income statement accounts to a zero value and transferring the total to retained earnings. Once this is done you are ready to process transactions for the new year.

These routines are supplemental to the regular daily work of writing checks, preparing sales invoices, preparing payroll, and other procedures. The only additional task is that of coding the transactions prior to posting them into the computer system; the coding process is different from that performed on a manual system.

Chart of Accounts

On most simple manual systems, the chart of accounts consists of a list of account titles, with the posting decision made based on the description of the transaction. On more sophisticated accounting systems and all computerized systems, the account code is numeric with a written description. Therefore, to code transactions, the written description of the transaction must be translated into its numeric equivalent.

An example of a chart of accounts with numeric codes is shown in Table 9 (Chapter 4). In the example, a check is made out to an insurance company for $50 for the monthly health insurance. The code for health insurance is 625, and the code for the checking account is 110. The check would then be coded to account 625. When entering the transactions at week's end, this check would be entered as one item in the cash disbursements journal to account 625 for a charge (debit) of $50. At the end of the posting of the cash disbursements journal, the sum of all the entries would be entered as credits to account 110 (cash in bank, checking account).

Once you have coded your accounts — see discussion on next page — you won't need to reenter the numbers. In most accounting systems, the input screen displays the title of an account as well as the account number. The computer uses the account number as the primary identifier when processing the data.

Most computer systems will not complete posting a journal unless debits equal credits. This is a simple type of control called balance control. In manual systems you are usually unable to determine if the accounting records are in balance without extracting a trial balance. Since this is usually some time after the posting has been made, it is more difficult to look back and determine where the error is. This is where good accounting controls can help you.

Valuable Tips

Much of what has been discussed relates to the procedures followed in day-to-day bookkeeping on a computerized system. The following are tips which will make your computerized accounting system easier to use.

Back up data

This quick and easy procedure can save weeks in recreating records should your system "crash." Data should be "backed up" (copies made) each time entries are made. If the computerized accounting system is used every day, the final final task of the day should be to back up the data. In addition, the entire system should be backed up at regular intervals, usually weekly or monthly. Should problems occur which cause the loss of data, having proper back-up means you should never have to manually input more than that one day's work.

Off-site storage

Keep an up-to-date set of back-up diskettes at your home or another location other than the office. In the event of a fire, copies of business records stored off-site can replace those that may have been damaged or destroyed.

Make copies of system disks

This is similar to backing up, except that it involves the system disk(s). Backing up the system ensures that even if something goes wrong you still have a system to use. However, if there is a problem and you have lost or misplaced the original system disk(s), the system is lost.

Read the system manual

The manuals supplied with the computer and software contain a vast amount of information. Considerable time and frustration can be saved by reading these manuals. In addition, many software manuals include training lessons which can make you proficient in the use of the program after a short period of time.

Code accounting entries first

Before you start entering your data, code all the entries. This may sound a little tedious, but computerized accounting systems are driven by numeric account codes. Separating the tasks of coding and entering data is a time-saving procedure.

Restrict use of your computer

If a number of people use the computer without supervision, there is the risk of accounting data being altered, even inadvertently, without the owner or manager being aware of it. Should this happen, it can take a considerable amount of time to correct the problem.

Avoid mistakes by taking breaks

Try not to enter data for overly-extended periods of time without taking breaks. Sitting in front of a computer screen for long periods of time is tiring on you and particularly on your eyes. Eye fatigue can lead to costly mistakes. Take short breaks about every 20 to 30 minutes — or whatever is comfortable — to relax your eyes and help restore concentration.

Try to "phase" your data entry

Inputting data is less of a chore if it is a regular part of the work routine, than it is when put off until the last minute.

Always finish what you start

There is almost nothing more difficult to do than start something, not finish it, then come back several days later and work out what had been done and what was still left to do. This is particularly true when entering data into a computerized system.

Check how the statements look

Once you feel that you have entered the data for a period, print out the financial statements. Then you can take a look and see if they make sense — that they show what you thought they would. If not, your regular control and review procedures can be focused in areas where you think there is a problem.

Try producing more and different analysis reports. These timely reports, if used properly, will give you tremendous up-to-date insights into your business.

Improving Your Accounting System

In summary, any form of automated bookkeeping system will help improve your accounting system. For most small businesses, unless they already own a computer, the best starting point is a one-write system, particularly for cash disbursements. As the volume of your transactions increases and the repetition and totaling of numbers becomes more and more burdensome, you should seriously consider moving to a computerized accounting system.

One final caution. If your manual accounting system does not work, it is highly unlikely that a computerized system will work any better. In this instance, the problem is usually the quality and timeliness of the data, not the system itself.

The intent of using automated accounting systems is to reduce the amount of time you spend recording and reporting the past, and to give you more time to make your business more profitable and successful. If used properly, an automated accounting system will also help give you quick information upon which to base your business decisions. You now have the ammunition for success.

Accounting Controls

The twofold objective of accounting controls is to

- help ensure that accounting data is entered correctly and
- help protect your assets.

Controls which help ensure that the accounting data is correctly entered are a form of processing control. These controls attempt to ensure that entries are in balance and that the resulting financial statements make sense.

The balance controls most commonly used are those that subtotal a batch of entries, post the entries, and check to verify that the total posted is the same as previously summed.

For systems that do not offer batch controls, try a simple cash control — your opening bank balance, plus deposits, less checks should equal your closing bank balance. When you compare your figures to the results generated by your entries into the system and the amounts agree, you will be sure that you have processed all the items.

Review and Reconciliation

Controls designed to ensure that financial statements make sense consist primarily of review and reconciliation procedures. The review procedures consist of reviewing detailed customer, supplier, inventory, and payroll subledgers, and income and expense account totals to determine that they make sense. Reconciliations consist of comparing the totals of accounts on the balance sheet and some income statement accounts to underlying detail to ensure that all entries have been posted correctly.

Review Control Examples

Joe Smith owes you $1,250 for goods shipped to him three months ago. You recall that these goods had been damaged in transit, were returned, and he was given credit for the shipment. In this case, the credit note may not have been posted to the accounting records. In addition, check to see that you had made the claim from the shipping company and been paid for the damage.

Similarly, an example of the effect of a reconciliation procedure used on a balance sheet account is that at the end of January a reconciliation of the bank statement shows that there should be $12,567.36 in the checking account. The general ledger balance at the end of the month, however, was $18,087.56. Upon investigation you find that January bank charges of $20.20 and a transfer of $5,500.00 to the money market account had not been posted to the accounting records.

An example of the effect of a reconciliation procedure on an income statement account is found in comparing the March sales total in the general ledger to the sales invoice total kept in a sales log. You find that the general ledger total for sales is $1,750.00 lower than the log total. On scrutinizing the sales journal posted to the general ledger, you discover that invoice 2376 to Brown Bros. is not included.

Most of the review and reconciliation controls are based on common sense, as you will see with the following example of the purchasing cycle which consists of all events that give rise to buying and paying for goods and services.

Table 13 – The Purchasing Cycle

Step	Control
Ordering	Goods cannot be ordered without approval. This can be achieved by always using purchase orders, which must be approved by you.
Receiving	Goods are not accepted unless the packing list agrees with a purchase order, and the goods are in good condition. At this point a receiving document is prepared.
Payment	No payment is made without an invoice (approved by the appropriate person), a receiving slip (indicating the goods were received in good condition), and a purchase order (indicating that the ordering was authorized and that the invoice price and quantities agree).

The Importance of Controls

All of these examples illustrate how errors can be detected by the use of control procedures and review. None of the errors would have been detected without controls and review, since the books were in balance. When maintaining accounting records, review will be an ongoing procedure as you do the work and reconciliation procedures will be part of your normal month-end routine. When someone else is maintaining the accounting records, however, it becomes very important to ensure that the monthly reconciliations are properly completed and that you personally conduct review procedures.

As more people are employed in your business, you will delegate not only work but responsibility. As this happens, it becomes important to establish sound accounting controls. Review procedures can help in some ways, such as in the example given above where you established that you had to claim the damage to a shipment from the shipping company. However, there are other control procedures that are specifically designed to ensure that cash is not spent without proper authorization and that you know what assets you have and where they are. These controls tend to be more functional and integrated into everyday work life.

These steps may seem bureaucratic, but they are vital in protecting your interests. When performed on a regular, timely basis, these steps are not excessively time consuming, and they can save you hard cash. Controls can prevent embarrassment, such as being accidentally overdrawn at the bank, when your records are accurate and up-to-date. These controls work just as well with the simplest manual accounting system as they do with the most sophisticated computerized system.

The need for accounting controls cannot stressed enough, particularly when you delegate work to your employees. To use sound accounting controls, even on an informal basis when you are the sole employee, is just good business and simply common sense.

The Accounting Cycle

Introduction to Examples

The purpose of this section is to illustrate the entire accounting cycle. Specific examples of transactions are given, these
source documents and nonpaper transactions are then posted
to the appropriate journals, the journals closed, and totals
posted to the general ledger. Finally, the data from the general

ledger is posted to the working trial balance sheet and the June 30, 19xx financial statements produced.

The example being used is a service company providing certain deposition services to the electronics industry. The service does not include the addition of any parts or components to the customer's product; therefore, there is no direct material cost to the company. The service provided consists of depositing certain gases onto the customer's unfinished product and then shipping this product to the customer. There are no sales taxes involved in the process. There are no cash sales, and sales are recognized by XYZ Services, Inc. at the time of shipment.

Look at the transaction examples shown below, then use these as a practice session and try to determine the appropriate entries — the double entries to the appropriate journal and the amounts. Then compare your answers with the following data which illustrates the entire cycle. By following this example you can trace the accounting entries from original journal entries to the final financial statements. The following transactions occurred in XYZ Services, Inc. during June.

Exhibit A-A – Check Transactions to the General Journal

Transaction Number	Date of Transaction	Description of Transaction
1	June 1	Paid check to Silicon Valley Realty the sum of $2,500 for June rent.
2	June 1	Received shipment of gas on open account from ABC Gas Company invoice amount of $2,000.
3	June 2	Shipped product to J & M Semicon, invoice nos. 2301 ($4,300), and 2302 ($2,200).
4	June 2	Paid check to InsurCo for Workers' Compensation insurance for June through August in the amount of $2,250.
5	June 3	Paid by check federal and state payroll taxes, federal amount of $4,500, and state amount of $950. These deposits were made for the pay period ended May 31, 19XX.
6	June 4	Shipped product to Dakota Semi, invoice no. 2303 ($5,950).
7	June 4	Received on open account, test wafers from Testco, invoice amount of $2,250.

Transaction Number	Date of Transaction	Description of Transaction
8	June 7	Paid check to Amtel for prior month telephone bill in the amount of $250.
9	June 7	Paid check to Utilities, Inc. for prior month electricity and water bill in the amount of $2,500.
10	June 7	Received check from Dakota Semi in the amount of $16,500 for payment on account.
11	June 9	Paid check to Susceptors, Ltd. in the amount of $2,200 on open account.
12	June 9	Received on open account, quartz from QuartzCo, invoice value of $1,100.
13	June 10	Shipped product to Nocar Micro, invoices no. 2304 ($7,200), no. 2305 ($2,750), and to J & M Semicon, invoices no. 2306 ($4,200) and no. 2307 ($3,300).
14	June 10	Paid check to JJ's Hardware for supplies to repair filter, invoice amount $375.
15	June 10	Paid check to Rentco, in the amount of $6,500, for equipment rental for June.
16	June 11	Received checks: $250 from Utilities, Inc. for a rebate on utility bill, and $17,500 from Elton, Ltd. payment on open account.
17	June 14	Paid check in the amount of $2,500 to Bank of XXX for May loan payment; $500 interest expense and $2,000 for principal repayment.
18	June 15	Paid checks for payroll period ending June 15, net checks in the amount of $8,200. (Note: See Payroll Register Example 1 for a detail of all checks.)
19	June 17	Received check from Uni Micro in the amount of $7,700, payment on open account.
20	June 18	Paid checks to the Bank of XXX (for the Internal Revenue Service) and State of California for payroll taxes withheld; $3,050 paid to the IRS, and $540 paid to the Employment Development Department (State of California) for the pay period ended June 15, 19XX.
21	June 18	Shipped product to Dakota Semi, invoices no. 2308 ($6,450) and no. 2309 ($2,750); and to Elton, Ltd. invoices no. 2310 ($6,400), no. 2311 ($2,100), and no. 2312 ($3,800).
22	June 22	Received delivery of gas on open account from ABC Gas Company, invoice value of $3,750.
23	June 23	Paid check for chemical delivery, COD, to Vapor, Inc. in the amount of $3,600.
24	June 24	Received check in the amount of $25,000 from John Smith, a new investor in the company; purchase of common stock.

Exhibit A-A – Check Transactions to the General Journal (continued)

Transaction Number	Date of Transaction	Description of Transaction
25	June 25	Shipped product to Dakota Semi, invoice no. 2313 ($11,500), and to Nocar Micro, invoices no. 2314 ($6,500) and no. 2315 ($5,750).
26	June 25	Purchased office supplies on account from Stationer's, Inc., invoice value $1,850.
27	June 25	Paid check to A & A Reps, company sales representatives, in the amount of $5,350 for May commissions.
28	June 29	Shipped product to EXEX Products, invoice no. 2316 ($9,500).
29	June 30	Paid checks for payroll period ending June 30, net amount of checks $9,500. (See Payroll Register Example 2 for detail of all checks.)
30	June 30	Received shipment on open account of chemicals from NACL, Inc., invoice value of $3,400.

In addition to these transactions, XYZ Services had several noncheck or invoice-related standard journal entries which were made in the general journal.

Exhibit A-B – Noncheck Transactions to the General Journal

Transaction Number	Description of Transaction
1	Insurance expense for June (should be one-third of June 2 payment to InsurCo). This entry is a derivative from check #76, which was a prepayment of insurance costs for three months. Since this payment was booked as a prepayment, a journal entry must be made to reflect the insurance costs for June.
2	Depreciation for June (see general journal, appropriate entry).
3	Interest accrual for June. Since no payment was made on the loan for the month of June: loan balance $40,000, annual interest rate of 12%.
4	Telephone and utility bills were not received in June at the closing date for June. Need to estimate bill for June and make a general journal entry. This accrual should be made for any significantly large invoice that you know relates to a given period, but which has not been received.
5	Accrued commission expense for the month of June (see general journal for appropriate entry).
6	The payroll-related entries are performed in the general journal in these examples. You may choose to perform these entries in a payroll journal. See general journal entries #6 and #7 for general journal treatment of payroll.

When booking payroll-related expenses, remember that there are two types of payroll taxes: employee taxes and employer taxes. The employee withholdings are clearly shown in the payroll ledgers. It is your responsibility to know the employer's payroll-related expenses and to book them properly. The employer's payroll taxes are detailed in the explanations below each general journal entry. To facilitate recording the above entries, the chart of accounts for XYZ Services, Inc., is shown below.

Exhibit A-C – Chart of Accounts

XYZ Services, Inc.
Chart of Accounts

Account Number	Account Description
100	Cash in Bank
105	Cash, in Investments
110	Accounts Receivable
120	Prepaid Insurance
150	Production Equipment
155	Accumulated Depreciation – Equipment
160	Leasehold Improvements
165	Accumulated Depreciation – Leasehold
180	Deposits
200	Accounts Payable
205	Commissions Payable
206	Payroll Payable
210	Payroll Taxes Payable (one or more accounts may be used for the various tax withholdings)
220	Loan Payable
225	Interest Payable
280	Income Taxes Payable
300	Common Stock
310	Retained Earnings – Prior Years
315	Retained Earnings – Current Year
400	Sales
500	Chemical Expense
505	Commission Expense
510	Depreciation Expense
515	Equipment Rent Expense

Exhibit A-C – Chart of Accounts (continued)

Account Number	Account Description
520	Gas Expense
522	Insurance Expense
525	Interest Expense
530	Office Expense
535	Other Miscellany
540	Payroll Expense
545	Quartz Expense
550	Rent Expense
555	Repairs & Maintenance Expense
560	Susceptors Expense
565	Telephone Expense
570	Test Wafer Expense
575	Utilities Expense
600	Income Tax Expense

Tracing the Entries – Some Exercises

At this point, you have sufficient information with which to trace through the appropriate entries for the transactions listed on the previous pages. Try to follow each entry and understand the logic behind the accounting treatment. Continue to walk through the entries until you understand them. The following two examples are payroll registers for periods ending June 15 and June 30.

Exhibits A-F through A-J on pages 130 to 133 demonstrate the posting of transactions — detailed at the beginning of this section — to the various journals. For instance, transaction number 11 can be seen in Exhibit A-F on line 7 coded as a debit to accounts payable and as a credit to cash in bank.

Once these journals have been prepared, the next step is to post all the entries for the month of June 19xx to the general ledger. This is demonstrated in Exhibit M in Chapter 4.

Exhibit A-D – Payroll Register: Example 1

XYZ Services, Inc.
Payroll Register
Period Ending June 15, 19xx

Name	Gross Salary	Federal			State		Net Salary
		W/H	FICA	Medicare	W/H	SDI	
Anne	$ 3,082.30	$ 390.00	$191.10	$ 44.69	$140.00	$27.00	$2,300.00
Joe	2,219.23	400.00	137.59	32.18	130.00	20.25	1,500.00
Mike	1,917.79	250.00	118.90	27.81	60.00	16.98	1,450.00
Steve	1,154.62	170.00*	71.59	16.74	40.00	10.13	850.00
Mary	1,510.70	230.00	93.66	21.91	50.00	13.99	1,100.00
John	1,047.63	150.00	64.95	15.19	20.00	8.31	·800.00
Sue	226.73	10.00	14.06	3.29	.08	1.78	200.00
Totals	$11,159.00	$1,600.00	$691.85	$161.81	$440.08	$98.44	$8,200.00

Exhibit A-E – Payroll Register: Example 2

XYZ Services, Inc.
Payroll Register
Period Ending June 30, 19xx

Name	Gross Salary	Federal			State		Net Salary
		W/H	FICA	Medicare	W/H	SDI	
Anne	$ 3,082.30	$ 390.00	$191.10	$ 44.69	$140.00	$ 27.00	$2,300.00
Joe	2,219.23	400.00	137.59	32.18	130.00	20.25	1,500.00
Mike	2,134.61	250.00	132.35	30.95	55.09	19.21	1,650.00
Steve	1,154.62	170.00	71.59	16.74	40.00	10.13	850.00
Mary	1,757.54	250.00	108.97	25.48	62.25	15.55	1,300.00
John	1,360.13	165.00	84.33	19.72	32.43	12.06	1,050.00
Sue	250.00	10.00	15.50	3.63	8.97	2.25	210.00
Emilio	835.24	110.00	51.78	12.11	15.25	7.26	640.00
Totals	$12,973.67	$1,745.00	$793.21	$185.50	$483.99	$113.71	$9,500.00

Note: The state payroll withholdings are based upon California taxes. Your state may not have the same tax structure. Additionally, some local governments have payroll-related taxes. Consult your local and state tax authorities for the specifics of your region before you set up a payroll register.

Exhibit A-F – Cash Disbursements Journal

XYZ Services, Inc.
Cash Disbursements Journal
Period: June 19XX

Date	Description	Check #	Cash #100 (Cr)	Gas Expense #520 (Dr)	Chemical Expense #500 (Dr)	Equip Rental #515 (Dr)	Repairs Expense #555 (Dr)	Rent Expense #555 (Dr)	Office Expense #530 (Dr)	Telephone Expense #565 (Dr)	Accounts Payable #200 (Dr)	P\R Tax Payable #210 (Dr)	Other Account	Other Amount (Dr)
6/1	Silicon Valley Realty	75	2,500.00					2,500.00						
6/2	InsurCo	76	2,250.00										120	2,250.00
6/3	IRS	77	4,500.00								4,500.00			
6/3	EDD (State of CA)	78	950.00								950.00			
6/7	Amtel	79	250.00								250.00			
6/7	Utilities, Inc.	80	2,500.00								2,500.00			
6/9	Susceptor's, Inc.	81	2,200.00								2,200.00			
6/10	JJ's Hardware	82	375.00				375.00							
6/10	RentCo	83	6,500.00			6,500.00								
6/14	Bank of XXX	84	2,500.00										220	2,000.00
													525	500.00
6/15	Payroll	85-91	8,200.00										206	8,200.00
6/15	Void	92	0.00											
6/18	IRS	93	3,050.00								3,050.00			
6/18	EDD (State of CA)	94	540.00								540.00			
6/23	Vapor, Inc.	95	3,600.00		3,600.00									
6/25	A & A Reps	96	5,350.00										205	5,350.00
6/30	Payroll	97-103	9,500.00										206	9,500.00
	June Total		54,765.00	0.00	3,600.00	6,500.00	375.00	2,500.00	0.00	0.00	4,950.00	9,040.00		27,800.00

Summary of Other Accounts

#120	2,250.00
#205	5,350.00
#206	17,700.00
#220	2,000.00
#525	500.00
	27,800.00

Exhibit A-G – Cash Receipts Journal

XYZ Services, Inc.
Cash Receipts Journal
Period: June 19XX

Date	Description	Cash #100 (Dr)	Acc Rec #110 (Cr)	Other Account	Other Amount (Cr)
6/7	Dakota Semi	16,500.00	16,500.00		
6/11	Utilities, Inc.	250.00		575	250.00
6/11	Elton, Ltd	17,500.00	17,500.00		
6/17	Uni Micro	7,700.00	7,700.00		
6/24	John Smith	25,000.00		300	25,000.00
	June Total	66,950.00	41,700.00		25,250.00

Summary of Other Entries

575	250.00
300	25,000.00
	25,250.00

Exhibit A-H – Purchases Journal

XYZ Services, Inc.
Purchases Journal
Period: June 19XX

Date	Description	Purchase Order	Accounts Payable #200 (Cr)	Gas Expense #520 (Dr)	Test Wafers #570 (Dr)	Chemical #500 (Dr)	Quartz #545 (Dr)	Susceptor #560 (Dr)	Office #530 (Dr)	Other Account	Other Amount (Dr)
6/1	ABC Gas Co.	55411	2,000.00	2,000.00							
6/4	TESTCO	55412	2,250.00		2,250.00						
6/9	QuartzCo	55416	1,100.00				1,100.00				
6/22	ABC Gas Co.	55415	3,750.00	3,750.00							
6/25	Stationer's Inc.	55417	1,850.00						1,850.00		
6/30	NACL, Inc.	55419	3,400.00			3,400.00					
	June Total		14,350.00	5,750.00	2,250.00	3,400.00	1,100.00	0.00	1,850.00		0.00

Exhibit A-I – Sales Journal

XYZ Services, Inc.
Sales Journal
Period: June 19XX

Date	Description	Invoice Number	Sales #400 (Cr)	Sales Tax Payable (Cr)	Acc Rec #110 (Dr)	Sales Tax Expense #500 (Dr)	Other Account	Other Amount (Cr)
6/2	J & M Semicon	2301	4,300.00		4,300.00			
6/2	J & M Semicon	2302	2,200.00		2,200.00			
6/4	Dakota Semi	2303	5,950.00		5,950.00			
6/10	Nocar Micro	2304	7,200.00		7,200.00			
6/10	Nocar Micro	2305	2,750.00		2,750.00			
6/10	J & M Semicon	2306	4,200.00		4,200.00			
6/10	J & M Semicon	2307	3,300.00		3,300.00			
6/18	Dakota Semi	2308	6,450.00		6,450.00			
6/18	Dakota Semi	2309	2,750.00		2,750.00			
6/18	Elton, Ltd	2310	6,400.00		6,400.00			
6/18	Elton, Ltd	2311	2,100.00		2,100.00			
6/18	Elton, Ltd	2312	3,800.00		3,800.00			
6/25	Dakota Semi	2313	11,500.00		11,500.00			
6/25	Nocar Micro	2314	6,500.00		6,500.00			
6/25	Nocar Micro	2315	5,750.00		5,750.00			
6/29	Exex, Inc.	2316	9,500.00		9,500.00			
	June Total		84,650.00	0.00	84,650.00	0.00		0.00

Exhibit A-J – General Journal

XYZ Services, Inc.
General Journal
Period: June 19XX

Page 1

Date	Account Number		Debit	Credit	Posted
6/30	1-	522	750.00		✓
		120		750.00	✓
			(To recognize Insurance Expense		
			for June; prepaid 3 months @		
			$750.00 per month; Check #76.)		
6/30	2-	510	2,750.00		✓
		155		2,000.00	✓
		165		750.00	✓
			(To recognize Depreciation		
			expense for June per Fixed Asset		
			Schedule.)		
6/30	3-	525	400.00		✓
		225		400.00	✓
			(To accrue Interest Expense		
			for June. Payment not made		
			as of 6/30; loan balance is		
			$40,000, interest rate is 12% per		
			annum.)		
6/30	4-	565	275.00		✓
		575	3,265.00		✓
		200		3,540.00	✓
			(To accrue estimated utility		
			and telephone bills for June.)		
6/30	5-	505	4,200.00		
		205		4,200.00	
			(To recognize commissions		
			earned, but not paid on June		
			Sales.)		

Exhibit A-J – General Journal (continued)

XYZ Services, Inc.
General Journal

Page 2

Date	Account Number	Debit	Credit	Posted
6/30	6- 540	12,448.00		✓
	210		4,248.00	✓
	206		8,200.00	✓
	(To expense Payroll and Payroll			
	Tax obligations; Payroll expense			
	includes employer's tax			
	obligations including FICA 820.48			
	FUTA 89.11, and State			
	Unemployment 379.41. Gross			
	Payroll data is in Payroll Register			
	for period ended June 15th.)			
6/30	7- 540	14,282.00		✓
	210		4,782.00	✓
	206		9,500.00	✓
	(To expense Payroll and Payroll			
	Tax obligations; employer's			
	tax obligations include			
	FICA 950.97, FUTA 102.68, and			
	State Unemployment 434.68.			
	See Payroll Register for period			
	ended June 30.)			

The general ledger — on the next page — is the heart of the accounting records of any company. By posting all the transactions for the month of June 19xx to the general ledger, the records of XYZ Services, Inc. are now up to date as of June 30, 19xx.

Exhibit A-K – General Ledger

XYZ Services, Inc.
General Ledger
Period: June 19XX

Date	Account Name \ #	Debit	Credit
	Cash in Bank #100		
5/31	Ending Balance	25,500.00	
6/30	June CDJ		54,765.00
6/30	June CRJ	66,950.00	
6/30	Ending Balance	37,685.00	
	Cash Investment #105		
5/31	Ending Balance	50,000.00	
6/30	June Activity	0.00	
6/30	Ending Balance	50,000.00	
	Accts Rec'ble #110		
5/31	Ending Balance	125,000.00	
6/30	June CRJ		41,700.00
6/30	June SJ	84,650.00	
6/30	Ending Balance	167,950.00	
	Prepaid Insur #120		
5/31	Ending Balance	0.00	
6/30	June CDJ	2,250.00	
6/30	June GJ (6-1)		750.00
6/30	Ending Balance	1,500.00	
	Equipment #150		
5/31	Ending Balance	120,000.00	
6/30	June Activity	0.00	
6/30	Ending Balance	120,000.00	
	Accum Depreciation		
	Equipment #155		
5/31	Ending Balance		34,000.00
6/30	June GJ (6-2)		2,000.00
6/30	Ending Balance		36,000.00

Exhibit A-K – General Ledger (continued)

XYZ Services, Inc.
General Ledger
Period: June 19XX

Date	Account Name \ #	Debit	Credit
	Leasehold #160		
5/31	Ending Balance	45,000.00	
6/30	June Activity	0.00	
6/30	Ending Balance	45,000.00	
	Accum Depreciation		
	Leasehold #165		
5/31	Ending Balance		12,750.00
6/30	June GJ (6-2)		750.00
6/30	Ending Balance		13,500.00
	Deposits #180		
5/31	Ending Balance	52,000.00	
6/30	June Activity	0.00	
6/30	Ending Balance	52,000.00	
	Accounts		
	Payable #200		
5/31	Ending Balance		7,500.00
6/30	June PJ		14,350.00
6/30	June CDJ	4,950.00	
6/30	June GJ (6-4)		3,540.00
	Ending Balance		20,440.00
	Commissions #205		
5/31	Ending Balance		4,750.00
6/30	June CDJ	5,350.00	
6/30	June GJ (6-5)		4,200.00
	Ending Balance		3,600.00
	Payroll Payable #206		
5/31	Ending Balance		0.00
6/30	June CDJ	17,700.00	
6/30	June GJ (6-6)		8,200.00
6/30	June GJ (6-7)		9,500.00
6/30	Ending Balance		0.00

Exhibit A-K – General Ledger (continued)

XYZ Services, Inc.
General Ledger
Period: June 19XX

Date	Account Name \ #	Debit	Credit
	Payroll Tax		
	Payable #210		
5/31	Ending Balance		6,200.00
6/30	CDJ-6	9,040.00	
6/30	June GJ (6-6)		4,248.00
6/30	June GJ (6-7)		4,782.00
6/30	Ending Balance		6,190.00
	Loan Payable #220		
5/31	Ending Balance		42,000.00
6/30	CDJ-6	2,000.00	
6/30	Ending Balance		40,000.00
	Interest Payble #225		
5/31	Ending Balance		0.00
6/30	June GJ (6-3)		4,000.00
6/30	Ending Balance		4,000.00
	Income Tax		
	Payable #280		
5/31	Ending Balance		35,160.00
6/30	June Closing Entry		7,482.00
6/30	Ending Balance		42,642.00
	Common Stock #300		
5/31	Ending Balance		47,400.00
6/30	CRJ-6		25,000.00
6/30	Ending Balance		72,400.00
	Retained Earnings		
	Prior #310		
5/31	June CDJ		175,000.00
6/30	June Activity		0.00
6/30	Ending Balance		175,000.00

Exhibit A-K – General Ledger (continued)

XYZ Services, Inc.
General Ledger
Period: June 19XX

Date	Account Name \ #	Debit	Credit
	Sales #400		
5/31	Ending Balance		410,000.00
6/30	SJ-6		84,650.00
6/30	Ending Balance		494,650.00
	Chemical Exp #500		
5/31	Ending Balance	12,500.00	
6/30	CDJ-6	3,600.00	
6/30	PJ-6	3,400.00	
6/30	Ending Balance	19,500.00	
	Commission Expense #505		
5/31	Ending Balance	21,000.00	
6/30	June GJ (6-5)	4,200.00	
6/30	Ending Balance	25,200.00	
	Depreciation Expense #510		
5/31	Ending Balance	13,750.00	
6/30	June GJ (6-2)	2,750.00	
6/30	Ending Balance	16,500.00	
	Equipment Rental Expense #515		
5/31	Ending Balance	35,500.00	
6/30	CDJ-6	6,500.00	
6/30	Ending Balance	42,000.00	
	Gas Expense #520		
5/31	Ending Balance	31,000.00	
6/30	PJ-6	5,750.00	
6/30	Ending Balance	36,750.00	

Exhibit A-K – General Ledger (continued)

XYZ Services, Inc.
General Ledger
Period: June 19XX

Date	Account Name \ #	Debit	Credit
	Insurance Exp #522		
5/31	Ending Balance	3,750.00	
6/30	June GJ (6-1)	750.00	
6/30	Ending Balance	4,500.00	
	Interest Exp #525		
5/31	Ending Balance	3,400.00	
6/30	CDJ-6	500.00	
6/30	June GJ (6-3)	400.00	
6/30	Ending Balance	4,300.00	
	Office Expense #530		
5/31	Ending Balance	4,500.00	
6/30	PJ-6	1,850.00	
6/30	Ending Balance	6,350.00	
.	Other Miscellaneous		
	Expense #535		
5/31	Ending Balance	750.00	
6/30	June Activity	0.00	
6/30	Ending Balance	750.00	
	Payroll #540		
5/31	Ending Balance	127,500.00	
6/30	June GJ (6-6)	12,448.00	
6/30	June GJ (6-7)	14,282.00	
6/30	Ending Balance	154,230.00	
	Quartz Exp #545		
5/31	Ending Balance	8,200.00	
6/30	PJ-6	1,100.00	
6/30	Ending Balance	9,300.00	

Exhibit A-K – General Ledger (continued)

XYZ Services, Inc.
General Ledger
Period: June 19XX

Date	Account Name \ #	Debit	Credit
	Rent Exp #550		
5/31	Ending Balance	13,500.00	
6/30	CDJ-6	2,500.00	
6/30	Ending Balance	16,000.00	
	Repairs & Maintenance #555		
5/31	Ending Balance	11,000.00	
6/30	CDJ-6	375.00	
6/30	Ending Balance	11,375.00	
	Susceptor Exp #560		
5/31	Ending Balance	9,500.00	
6/30	June Activity	0.00	
6/30	Ending Balance	9,500.00	
	Telephone Expense #565		
5/31	Ending Balance	2,750.00	
6/30	June GJ (6-4)	275.00	
6/30	Ending Balance	3,025.00	
	Test Wafers #570		
5/31	Ending Balance	8,750.00	
6/30	PJ-6	2,250.00	
6/30	Ending Balance	11,000.00	
	Utilities Exp #575		
5/31	Ending Balance	14,750.00	
6/30	CRJ-6		250.00
6/30	June GJ (6-4)	3,265.00	
6/30	Ending Balance	17,765.00	

Exhibit A-K – General Ledger (continued)

XYZ Services, Inc.
General Ledger
Period: June 19XX

Date	Account Name \ #	Debit	Credit
	Income Tax		
	Expense #600		
5/31	Ending Balance	35,160.00	
6/30	June Closing Entry	7,482.00	
6/30	Ending Balance	42,642.00	

You may have noticed that all the entries in the general ledger have references or descriptions in addition to the date and amount. These are the posting references which act as an audit trail, enabling you to look at the general ledger and trace any entry back to its source documents. For instance, we noted earlier how transaction number 11 was included in the cash disbursements journal (Exhibit A-F). If you now look at accounts payable, Account #200, you will see that the debit entry from the cash disbursements journal is $4,950. This is the same as the total checks coded to accounts payable in the cash disbursements journal (Exhibit A-F).

Similarly, you can trace all the journals to the general ledger accounts and thus see the accounting process flow.

Once the general ledger is posted, it is time to prepare the working trial balance. This will determine that our general ledger is in balance. This is the starting point for us to prepare financial statements. This is shown in Exhibit A-M.

The next schedule and closing journal entry were necessary to complete the closing of the books for XYZ Services, Inc. for the June period. Like most closing adjustments, they cannot be calculated until the working trial balance is posted and a preliminary net income calculated. In many instances, a draft set of financial statements is prepared, then the closing adjustments are calculated and the books closed for the period. This is much easier to do if you are maintaining your books on a computerized system than it is to do manually.

Exhibit A-L – Closing Journal Tax Calculations

XYZ Services, Inc.
Closing Journal Calculation of Taxes
for the Period June 19xx

Calculation of Pre-Tax Income:

Sales (Acct. #400)	$494,650
Expenses (Sum of Accts. #500–575)	388,045
Pre-Tax Income	$106,605

Calculation of Tax Provision:

Pre-Tax Income	$106,605
Anticipated Tax Rate	40%
Tax	$ 42,642

Calculation of Net Income:

Pre-Tax Income	$106,605
Tax	42,642
Net Income	$ 63,963

Calculation Of Closing Journal Required:

Tax Expense, As Calculated	$ 42,642
Tax Previously Provided (Acct. #600)	35,160
Adjustment Required	$ 7,482

XYZ Services, Inc.
Closing Journal Calculation of Taxes
For The Period June 19XX

Account	Acct. #	Debit	Credit
Income Taxes Payable	280		$7,482
Income Tax Expense		600	$7,482

Note: See attached Closing Journal Schedule for calculation supporting this journal [above].

Exhibit A-M – Working Trial Balance

XYZ Services, Inc.
Working Trial Balance
Period: June 19XX

Account Description	Account Number	Prior Period Balance Debit	Prior Period Balance Credit	General Ledger Bal Debit	General Ledger Bal Credit
Cash in Bank	100	25,500.00		37,685.00	
Cash, Investments	105	50,000.00		50,000.00	
Accounts Receivable	110	125,000.00		167,950.00	
Prepaid Insurance	120	0.00		1,500.00	
Production Equipment	150	120,000.00		120,000.00	
Accumulated Depreciation	155		34,000.00		36,000.00
Leasehold Improvements	160	45,000.00		45,000.00	
Accumulated Depreciation	165		12,750.00		13,500.00
Deposits	180	52,000.00		52,000.00	
Accounts Payable	200		7,500.00		20,440.00
Commissions Payable	205		4,750.00		3,600.00
Payroll Payable	206		0.00		0.00
Payroll Tax Payable	210		6,200.00		6,190.00
Loan Payable	220		42,000.00		40,000.00
Interest Payable	225		0.00		400.00
Income Tax Payable	280		35,160.00		35,160.00
Common Stock	300		47,400.00		72,400.00
Retained Earnings:					
-Prior Year	310		175,000.00		175,000.00
-Current Year	315		0.00		0.00
Sales	400		410,000.00		494,650.00
Chemical Expense	500	12,500.00		19,500.00	
Sales Commission Expense	505	21,000.00		25,200.00	
Depreciation Expense	510	13,750.00		16,500.00	
Equipment Rental Expense	515	35,500.00		42,000.00	
Gas Expense	520	31,000.00		36,750.00	
Insurance Expense	522	3,750.00		4,500.00	
Interest Expense	525	3,400.00		4,300.00	
Office Expense	530	4,500.00		6,350.00	
Other \ Miscellaneous Expense	535	750.00		750.00	
Payroll Expense	540	127,500.00		154,230.00	
Quartz Expense	545	8,200.00		9,300.00	
Rent Expense	550	13,500.00		16,000.00	
Repairs & Maintenance Expense	555	11,000.00		11,375.00	
Susceptors Expense	560	9,500.00		9,500.00	
Telephone Expense	565	2,750.00		3,025.00	
Test Wafer Expense	570	8,750.00		11,000.00	
Utilities Expense	575	14,750.00		17,765.00	
Income Tax Expense	600	35,160.00		35,160.00	
Totals		774,760.00	774,760.00	897,340.00	897,340.00

Closing Adjust		Income Statement		Balance Sheet	
Debit	Credit	Debit	Credit	Debit	Credit
				37,685.00	
				50,000.00	
				167,950.00	
				1,500.00	
				120,000.00	
					36,000.00
				45,000.00	
					13,500.00
				52,000.00	
					20,440.00
					3,600.00
					0.00
					6,190.00
					40,000.00
					400.00
	7,482.00				42,642.00
					72,400.00
					175,000.00
		63,963.00			63,963.00
			494,650.00		
		19,500.00			
		25,200.00			
		16,500.00			
		42,000.00			
		36,750.00			
		4,500.00			
		4,300.00			
		6,350.00			
		750.00			
		154,230.00			
		9,300.00			
		16,000.00			
		11,375.00			
		9,500.00			
		3,025.00			
		11,000.00			
		17,765.00			
7,482.00		42,642.00			
7,482.00	7,482.00	494,650.00	494,650.00	474,135.00	474,135.00

The working trial balance, shown in Exhibit A-M, contains a great number of figures. It may be helpful to quickly identify their sources.

Column 1 is the account code for each account. Columns 2 and 3 are the balance for each account at May 31, 19xx — the end of the previous period. Note that these are the same as the ending balance for each account in the general ledger (Exhibit K) at May 31, 19xx.

Columns 4 and 5 are the closing balances extracted directly from the general ledger. The final closing adjustment for taxes, detailed in Exhibit A-L, is included in columns 7 and 8.

The final balances for each account are then recorded depending upon whether the balance is a debit or a credit and whether the account relates to the income statement or the balance sheet in columns 9 through 12.

The Financial Statements

Once the working trial balance is complete, the financial statements can be prepared. These are shown in Exhibits A-N and A-O. Once you have reached this point, you have worked your way through the entire accounting cycle, have produced your financial statements, and can now look at them analytically, as demonstrated in Appendix II.

Exhibit A-N – Balance Sheet

XYZ Services, Inc.
Balance Sheet
June 30, 19xx

Assets

Cash in Bank	$ 37,685	
Cash in Investments	50,000	
Accounts Receivable	167,950	
Prepaid Insurance	1,500	
Total Current Assets		$257,135
Production Equipment	120,000	
Accumulated Depreciation – Equipment	(36,000)	
Leasehold Equipment	45,000	
Accumulated Depreciation – Leasehold	(13,500)	
Total Fixed Assets		115,500
Deposits		52,000
Total Assets		$424,635

Liabilities

Accounts Payable	$ 20,440	
Commissions Payable	3,600	
Payroll Payable	0	
Payroll Taxes Payable	6,190	
Loan Payable	40,000	
Interest Payable	400	
Income Taxes Payable	42,642	
Total Current Liabilities		$113,272

Equity

Common Stock	$ 72,400	
Retained Earnings – Prior	175,000	
Retained Earnings – Current	63,963	
Total Equity		$311,363
Total Liabilities & Equity		$424,635

Exhibit A-O – Income Statement

XYZ Services, Inc.
Statement of Income
Period Ending June 30, 19xx

Sales		$494,650
Expenses:		
Chemicals	$ 19,500	
Sales Commissions	25,200	
Depreciation Expense	16,500	
Equipment Rental	42,000	
Gas Expense	36,750	
Insurance Expense	4,500	
Interest Expense	4,300	
Office Expense	6,350	
Other Miscellaneous	750	
Payroll Expense	154,230	
Quartz Expense	9,300	
Rent Expense	16,000	
Repairs and Maintenance	11,375	
Susceptors Expense	9,500	
Telephone Expense	3,025	
Test Wafer Expense	11,000	
Utilities Expense	17,765	
Total Expenses		$388,045
Net Operating Profit		$106,605
Income Tax Expense		42,642
Net Income		$ 63,963

Financial Analysis Tools

Source Materials

The purpose of Appendix II is to illustrate the various financial analytic tools explained in Chapter 3. For continuity, the financial statements — the Balance Sheet and the Income Statement — generated in Appendix I have been used as the sources for the analyses and the basis for the explanations.

Percentage-of-Sales Analysis

The percentage of sales for each expense item in the income statement is shown to the side of each item in the income statement for XYZ Services, Inc. (opposite). Much can be seen from these numbers.

From these numbers you can calculate that each dollar of sales contributes 53.7 cents toward profit and other costs after paying for 46.3 cents of direct costs of sales. This is a healthy gross margin, since it permits a considerable drop in sales volume before XYZ Services, Inc. would start to show losses and feel cash shortage problems.

Similarly, you can tell that fixed overhead is relatively low and only a small amount of sales is required to pay the fixed operating costs of $90,400. Normally, you would compare the above percentages with those from previous periods to determine if trends were developing or changing. This is extremely useful both in helping you understand the dynamics of your business as well as being critical in assisting you prepare a budget for your business planning.

Exhibit A-P – Income Statement with Percentage of Sales

XYZ Services, Inc.
Statement of Income
Period Ending June 30, 19XX

	Sales	Percentage of Sales	Code
Sales	$494,650	100.0	
Less Expenses			
Chemicals	19,500	3.9	a
Sales Commissions	25,200	5.1	b
Depreciation Expense	16,500	3.3	c
Equipment Rental	42,000	8.5	c
Gas Expense	36,750	7.4	a
Insurance Expense	4,500	0.9	c
Interest Expense	4,300	0.8	c
Office Expense	6,350	1.3	c
Other Miscellany	750	0.2	c
Payroll Expense	154,230	31.2	a
Quartz Expense	9,300	1.9	a
Rent Expense	16,000	3.4	c
Repairs & Maintenance	11,375	2.3	d
Susceptors Expense	9,500	1.9	a
Telephone Expense	3,025	0.6	d
Test Wafer Expense	11,000	2.2	b
Utilities Expense	17,765	3.6	d
Total Expenses	388,045	78.5	
Net Operating Profit	$106,605	21.5	
Income Tax Expense	42,642	8.6	
Net Income	$ 63,963	12.9	

a = Direct cost of sales (Total $229,280, or 46.3% of sales)
b = Selling and promotion costs (Total $36,200, or 7.3% of sales)
c = Fixed general and administrative costs (Total $90,400 or 18.4% of sales)
d = Semivariable general and administrative costs (Total $32,165 or 6.5% of sales)

Ratio Analyses of Financial Statements

Using the figures from your income statement analysis, there are several different ratios that you can apply to gauge the health and viability of your business.

Creditability ratios

The significance of these two ratios relates to vendor creditworthiness. The ratios for XYZ Services, Inc. are very favorable, so the company should have no difficulty obtaining vendor credit.

Current ratio = 2.27

Since any current ratio greater than 2:1 is favorable, the company has an attractive current ratio.

Quick ratio = 2.26

Since any quick ratio greater than 1:1 is favorable, the company is extremely liquid.

Liquidity ratio

This ratio is also a liquidity ratio, however, the information is important internally. An index of the creditworthiness of your customers, or an evaluation of your collection efforts.

Average collection period = 61 Days

The company is taking two months to collect its accounts receivables. This is bad! An analysis of these accounts should be done to determine if there is a companywide problem.

Profitability ratios

These three ratios analyze the profitability of the company in terms that allow comparison with other types of investments. The returns for this company are very solid and imply that further investment in the company is not unwarranted.

Return on equity = 177%

Since Treasury Bills have a return of somewhere between 5–6%, this is a tremendous return on invested capital. Nice business!

Return on assets = 30%

The return on assets is a more complete measure of efficiency. It defines the return on all assets employed in the business, a return on reinvested capital and debt. Thirty percent is still nice!

Profit to net worth = 41%

The profit-to-net-worth ratio is a measure of your return on invested and reinvested capital. Forty-one percent is great!

Investment return ratios

These ratios demonstrate the company's ability to reward investors with a return on their investment. This is important to the company's lender (usually a bank) which wants to be repaid in full with interest, as well as to the owners of the company who will see the financial rewards for risking their money in the company and the additional rewards for their personal efforts.

Net profit on sales = 12.9%

Any net-profit-on-sales percentage above 10% is very attractive. It implies a very efficient operation.

Debt to net worth = 36%

A 100% debt-to-net-worth ratio means that the company is funded equally between debt and equity. The 36% figure means that more credit can be obtained.

Times interest earned = 26 times

The company is well able to meet its debt obligations.

Total debt to total assets = 27%

A 27% debts-to-assets ratio is generally very good.

These investment return ratios also show the company to be in a very solid financial position. It should be able to attract additional debt if needed.

Accounting Terms

ACCOUNT
ACCOUNT CODES
ACCOUNTANT
ACCOUNTING
ACCOUNTING CYCLE
ACCOUNTING PERIOD
ACCOUNTING SYSTEM
ACCOUNTS PAYABLE
ACCOUNTS RECEIVABLE
ACCRUAL METHOD
ACCRUAL EXPENSES
ADJUSTING JOURNAL ...

$

Account

One of a series of descriptions under which similar types of financial transactions are grouped, such as, Cash and Accounts Payable.

Account codes

The numeric representation of an account description in a chart of accounts, for example: 100 – Cash in bank.

Accountant

A person who works with financial data. This term is often used to describe a bookkeeper, but more often is used to describe a person with professional qualifications, such as a Certified Public Accountant (CPA).

Accounting

The overall process of recording and reporting financial transactions.

Accounting cycle

The process of entering all financial transactions and producing the financial statements for an accounting period.

Accounting period

A period of time, such as a month, a year, or a quarter, covered by any set of financial statements, particularly the income statement.

Accounting system

The structure under which financial data is processed, financial records are maintained, and financial reports produced.

Accounts payable

Amounts which you owe to your suppliers and other creditors for goods or services which you have received, but have not yet paid for.

Accounts receivable

Invoices which you have billed for goods delivered or services performed, but which your customers have not yet paid you for.

Accrual method

The method of accounting where income and expenses are recognized when they arise and not necessarily when they are received or paid.

Accrued expenses

Costs which have been incurred but have not yet been paid.

Adjusting journal

A series of entries made to the accounting records to adjust previously entered data.

Analysis

The process of reviewing and evaluating financial information.

Application program

A software program that processes data on a computer in usable form, such as an accounting software package.

Asset

An item of value which is the property of a business — cash, equipment, or buildings.

Audit

An examination of the business records. An external audit is performed by independent CPAs, who give their opinion on the financial statements of the business. Other types of audit include those by regulatory agencies, such as the Internal Revenue Service, and internal audits, conducted by employees of a business whose task it is to monitor certain aspects of the business' financial function.

Audit trail

The descriptions that enable one to track any transaction in the accounting records back to the original source data or document. See also: Posting reference.

Audited financial statements

Financial statements that have been audited by independent CPAs and include their audit opinion.

Back-up

The process of copying data stored on a computerized system onto removable media, such as floppy disks, magnetic tape, or CD, as a standby in case the original data is damaged or lost.

Balance sheet

A financial statement that shows assets, liabilities, and owner's equity at a specific point in time.

Batch processing

The process of inputting a series of transactions into a computerized accounting system and then comparing control totals to ensure that all data has been entered.

Beginning balance

The account balance at the beginning of a period. Sometimes also called balance carried forward.

Bonding

The process of obtaining a performance or other type of bond from an insurance company or surety.

Bookkeeper

The person who records data in the accounting records and maintains the accounting system.

Bookkeeping

The process of entering data in the accounting records and maintenance of the accounting system.

Budgeting

The process of projecting financial results for a future period.

Business liability insurance

A type of insurance that protects a business from the costs of improper business activities.

Capital

The amount of money invested and reinvested into a business by the owners. It is also called equity or net worth.

Cash basis

The method of accounting that recognizes income and expense

when cash is paid or received, not when earned or incurred. It can result in erratic income patterns and is generally used only by the smallest businesses.

Cash disbursements

The payment of cash for expenses or for the acquisition of assets by a business.

Cash flow statement

A statement that shows the sources and uses of cash. This is often a statement of projected cash flows, rather than an analysis of historic cash flow.

Cash receipts

Cash received by a business, usually from the sale of products or services.

Central processing unit (CPU)

The "core" of a computer, which processes data electronically.

Certified Public Accountant (CPA)

A person who has received extensive training in accounting and is licensed by the state to practice accounting. CPAs most commonly work in the fields of audit, tax, and management consulting.

Chart of accounts

A numbered list of account descriptions.

Closing

The process of finalizing the accounting records and producing the financial statement at the end of a business' accounting period.

Closing the books

The process of conducting the closing of the financial records at the end of an accounting period.

Comparative analysis

The process of comparing the results of a business for one or more time periods, or comparing the business with another business.

Compiled financial statements

Financial statements prepared by independent CPAs with their report stating the extent of their work.

Computer

A piece of electronic equipment that processes data and produces reports from that data. Also used to describe the "box" that contains the central processing unit (CPU) and other related hardware.

Computerized system

An accounting system maintained electronically on a computer.

Control

A procedure designed to protect assets and reduce the incidence of errors in the financial records of a business.

Control total

The total dollar value of a series of transactions to be posted to the accounting records. Once the entries have been made, the posted total is compared to the control total to ensure that all items have been posted. Control totals are most commonly used as part of batch processing.

Controller

The accountant who oversees the accounting function and has direct responsibility for closing the books and preparing financial statements.

Corporation

A form of business that is incorporated under state laws with limited liability. The name of a corporation is usually followed by "Incorporated" or "Inc." This is the most common form of business entity.

Cost of goods sold

See Cost of sales.

Cost of sales

The amount paid to buy or produce goods sold. This consists of direct costs only and excludes related selling and administrative costs. It is also called cost of goods sold.

Credit

An accounting term describing the sign of a transaction. Examples of credits are liabilities, sales, and capital. To increase the amount of a liability, or to decrease a debit balance (an asset), a credit is entered to the respective account. The term credit is also used to describe when a supplier gives a business extended payment terms, or extends credit.

Credit bureau

An entity whose business is to collect data about the credit history of a large number of businesses and individuals and then sell this information to businesses which evaluate potential customers, such as TRW and Dun & Bradstreet.

Credit terms

The payment terms given by a supplier to his customer; for example: Net 30 Days, which means payment is due within 30 days without any discount.

Creditors

The entities to whom you owe money.

Current assets

Assets which are expected to be converted into cash within the next year. Examples are inventory and, of course, cash itself.

Current liabilities

Debts that a business is obliged to pay within the next year. Examples are accounts payable, such as suppliers, and taxes.

Current ratio

This ratio measures a business' ability to pay its current liabilities from its current assets. The formula is:

$$\frac{\text{Total current assets}}{\text{Total current liabilities}}$$

The greater this ratio is over 1:1, the stronger a business is, and conversely, when less than 1:1, the greater the likelihood that a business is insolvent.

Customer

The key to any business' success, the person who buys your products or services.

Data

The numeric effect of business transactions, entered into an accounting system.

Debit

An accounting term describing the sign of a transaction. Examples are assets and expenses. Debit entries increase asset accounts and decrease credit (liability) accounts.

Debt

An amount owed by a business.

Debt capacity

The ability of a business to borrow money and to make loan payments together with interest on the due dates.

Debt coverage

The ability of a business to service its debt from its operations.

Debt to equity ratio

The total amount of liabilities divided by equity.

Debt to net worth ratio

Another term used to describe the Debt to Equity Ratio.

Debtors

People who owe you money. In a business these are often referred to as accounts receivable or receivables.

Deficit

An excess of expenses over income, or liabilities over assets.

Deposit in transit

Cash or checks deposited in the bank that have yet to clear and be recorded on the bank statement.

Depreciation

Allocation of the cost of an asset to operations over the term of the asset's useful life. There are often significant differences between depreciation recorded on the books and that indicated in a tax return.

Direct costs

Costs that are incurred solely in producing a business' products or services. Often called cost of sales.

Direct labor

The cost of labor that is used solely to produce a business' product or service.

Direct material

The cost of materials that are used solely to produce a business' product.

Discretionary cost

A cost that is not necessary to produce a product or service, but which may improve sales — sales promotions or improvements in other area of business life, such as pension and health plans.

Diskette

A medium for storing electronic data from a computerized system — usually a floppy, rigid, or compact disk.

Dividends

A cash distribution to the owners of a corporation. It represents an allocation of a portion of the business' cumulative profits.

Double entry

The basis of bookkeeping, where the sum of the debits equals the sum of the credits, and for each debit entry there is an equal credit entry.

Earnings per share

The single most important measure used by investors in determining the price of a company's shares. Earnings per share is calculated as follows:

$$\frac{\text{Net income}}{\text{Number of common shares outstanding}}$$

Ending balance

The balance in an account at the end of an accounting period, after all closing entries have been processed and totalled.

Entry

An individual transaction as recorded in the accounting records. Also, the process of recording transactions.

Equity

The amount owners have invested in a business. Also known as capital or net worth.

Expense

The use or expiration of the value of an asset. Cash is the most commonly used asset where it has been used to pay for a cost of the business. Expense reduces net income.

External users

People not employed by a business who read and rely on the financial statements and reports of that business in making their own business or investment decisions, such as creditors.

Finance

The subject of the management of funds. Also used to express when a business borrows money for the acquisition of assets or to fund operations.

Financial accounting

The branch of accounting concerned with the recording of financial transactions and the reporting of these through financial statements.

Financial statements

Reports (in a recognized format) that give information about the financial affairs of a business. The most common examples are the balance sheet and the income statement.

Fixed asset schedule

A listing of the fixed assets of a business together with their cost and depreciation.

Fixed assets

A long-lived asset, such as land, buildings, and equipment.

Fixed cost

A cost that remains static regardless of changes in sales volume. In reality, fixed costs tend to remain static for a given range of volume.

Formula

The mathematical instructions for calculating given items. For instance, the formula for calculating the current ratio is:

$$\frac{\text{Total current assets}}{\text{Total current liabilities}}$$

Funds flow statement

A financial statement that lists the sources and uses of funds for a business for a specified period of time.

General and administrative expenses

Costs incurred in managing a business as opposed to manufacturing a product or selling the product; these expenses are also sometimes referred to as overhead. Examples are office rent and administrative salaries.

General journal

A multipurpose journal used as a source for entering transactions into the accounting records. This is often used for entering noncash transactions such as depreciation.

General ledger

The principal book or ledger in an accounting system. This contains the history of all the transactions of the business.

Generally accepted accounting principles

The underlying theories and rules under which financial statements are prepared.

Generally accepted auditing standards

The standards under which CPAs perform audits and report on the financial statements of businesses.

Gross profit margin

The amount by which sales revenues exceed the direct costs of goods sold.

Hardware

A term usually used to describe physical computer equipment, such as the computer, monitor, and printer.

Historical information

Financial information prepared for an accounting period that has already ended.

In balance

Where the sum of the debits equal the sum of the credits. Sometimes also expressed as "the books balancing."

Income

Revenues derived from the sale of products and services or from the use of assets, such as interest on cash balances. See also: Net income (income after all expenses).

Income statement

The financial statement that relates costs and expenses and derives net income or net loss. This is often called the statement of profit and loss or the "P&L."

Industry averages

Statistical data compiled for financial attributes from a variety of businesses in a particular industry. These are used to compare the performance of a business against the average for its competitors.

Input device

A term used to describe the keyboard and mouse or track ball the operator uses to communicate with a computer.

Integrated modules

Subsystems often contained in accounting software packages that handle accounts payable, accounts receivable, and/or payroll. Entries to these subsystems are made directly and not through the general ledger. The accounting software accumulates the input data and posts it directly to the general ledger.

Interest

The cost of borrowing money. It is usually quoted as an annual rate.

Interim financial statements

Financial statements prepared for a business for a period other than its fiscal year.

Inventory

The stock of products held by a business. In manufacturing businesses, this is often split into such categories as raw materials, work in process, and finished goods.

Inventory turnover

The rate at which inventory moves in and out of a business. The inventory turnover rate is usually calculated by dividing the cost of goods sold (cost of sales) for the period by the average inventory for the period. The longer the period used, the more useful the result.

Investment

The amount of money expended in acquiring an asset. Also used to describe the asset so acquired. Stocks and bonds are often referred to as investments.

Investor

One who expends money to acquire an asset. For many businesses these are the people who provided the initial or expansion capital for the business.

Invoices

Bills sent to customers for payment for goods or services they have received.

Joint venture

A form of business organization similar to a partnership and is formed for the purpose of engaging in one particular business transaction or for a limited period of time.

Journal

The source of entry to the financial records where a series of similar transactions are assembled for bulk posting.

Kilobyte (K)

A measure of memory in a computer system which equals 1,000 bytes of data.

Law of physics

There are several laws of physics, such as the law of gravity, but one in particular applies to the business arena: "Every action has an equal and opposite reaction." In accounting, this is the case where every debit generates an equal credit.

Lease

A form of agreement for the use of buildings or equipment owned by others.

Ledger

An older term to describe a book of account, most usually found in the term "general ledger."

Leverage

The use of debt to acquire an asset.

Liability

An amount owed by a business — an accounts payable.

Liquidity

The flexibility that a business has by being able to convert assets into cash quickly.

Long-term liabilities

Debts that are due to be paid more than one year from the date shown on a balance sheet.

Loss

An excess of expenses over income.

Management

The people who run businesses.

Manual system

An accounting system maintained by hand, using pen and paper.

Manuals

Books prepared by computer and software manufacturers to instruct you in the use of their products.

Media

The term used to describe electronic data storage materials.

Megabyte (MB)

A measure of memory in a computer system which equals one million bytes of data.

Merchandise inventory

The stock of products routinely sold by a business, usually a retail business.

Monitor

The television screen-like object used to display information from a computer system.

Net assets

The excess of total assets less total liabilities. This is also referred to as equity.

Net income

The surplus of revenues and other income over expenses for an accounting period. Also called net profit.

Net loss

The opposite of net income, where expenses exceed income for an accounting period.

Net profit on sales

Usually expressed as the ratio of net profit divided by net sales.

Net worth

See Capital.

Nonrecurring transactions

Transactions that are unusual and not part of the day-to-day operations of a business.

Off-site storage

The practice of keeping a back-up copy of computerized data at another physical location.

One-write system

A pegboard-like duplicating system that allows details to be recorded on two documents at the same time. The most commonly found system is for checks, where the details are copied (by a carbon copy strip on the back of the check) onto a cash disbursements ledger or journal.

Opening balance

The balance in an account before any entries are made for the current accounting period.

Operating expenses

Costs incurred by a business in its day-to-day operations — rent, materials, wages.

Operating system

The software that operates the computer hardware.

Operations

The actual day-to-day activities of a business.

Out-of-balance

Where the sum of the debits does not equal the sum of the credits in the accounting records.

Out-of-balance edits

Controls found in accounting software packages which stop the system until the entries are in balance. They are designed to help detect and prevent clerical input errors.

Outstanding check

A check that has been issued by the payer but has yet to clear the bank and be included on the bank statement.

Overhead

Indirect expense. Although overhead is necessary, it cannot be specifically identified as a discrete cost in a business' finished product or service. See: General and administrative expenses.

Owner's equity

See Capital.

Partnership

A form of business entity where two or more investors own a business in an unincorporated form.

Payables

Amounts owed to suppliers and other creditors of a business, also called accounts payable.

Payables journal

The journal that accumulates entries from creditors' invoices for posting to the accounting records.

Payroll

Wages and salaries for employees, including state and federal payroll taxes.

Percentage-of-sales analysis

Where every line of an income statement is stated in its percentage term of sales.

Peripherals

Computer hardware, such as printers and external disk drives.

Planning

The process of anticipating the future based upon your business experience to date.

Posting

The process of entering transactions into the accounting records.

Posting reference

A symbol or abbreviation that refers to the source by which an entry was posted to the accounting records. This is an integral part of an effective audit trail.

Prepaid expenses

Expenses that have been paid but have an unexpired period of benefit, such as insurance premiums.

Price-earnings ratio

The market price of a stock divided by its earnings per share.

Price-earnings multiple

The price earnings ratio is expressed as an absolute number.

Product costs

Costs incurred directly in manufacturing a product.

Production expenses

The direct costs of production for a period.

Profit

The difference between revenue and cost, this is usually stated before interest and taxes.

Profit and loss statement

See Income Statement.

Profit margin

The excess of revenue for a single item over the direct product costs and attributable selling and delivery expenses.

Projections

Part of forming a plan by anticipating future revenues and expenses.

Purchase order

A document sent to a supplier that indicates that an order placed by a business is properly approved.

Purchasing cycle

The review and reconciliation controls established for ordering, receiving, and paying for goods and services.

Quick ratio

This ratio measures the liquidity of a business, and is also referred to as the acid test ratio. It is calculated by the following formula:

$$\frac{\text{Cash + marketable securities + accounts receivable}}{\text{Current liabilities}}$$

The typical minimum quick ratio is 1:1 for a healthy business.

Ratio

A number that results from dividing one value by another.

Ratio analysis

This type of analysis gives you the ability to interpret the relationships between values in a set of financial statements, both for a business itself and as compared with industry statistics.

Raw materials

The components that are manufactured or assembled into a business' finished products.

Receivables

Amounts due from customers and other debtors, usually for the sale of goods or services.

Receivables journal

The journal that accumulates entries from sales invoices for posting to the accounting records.

Reconciliation

The process of comparing the balance of an account with an external source to determine that the account balance is accurate. The most common example is a bank account reconciliation.

Recurring transactions

The normal day-to-day transactions of a business, such as sales, purchases, cash receipts, cash disbursements, and payroll.

Research and development expenses

The amounts expended on developing new products.

Retail

Where goods or services are sold direct to the public, such as a department store.

Retained earnings

Cumulative profits from prior periods that have not been distributed as dividends.

Return on assets

A ratio that measures how effectively a business manages its assets in generating profits. This is calculated as follows:

$$\frac{\text{Net profit}}{\text{Total assets}}$$

Return on equity

A ratio that measures the effective rate of return earned on the capital of the business. This is calculated as follows:

$$\frac{\text{Net profit}}{\text{Equity}}$$

Return on investment

A variety of ratios that express the cash flow generated by a segment of a business, or an investment, relative to the amount of money tied up to fund it.

Review

The process of reading financial information analytically, and asking the key question "Does it make sense?" Also a form of opinion issued by independent CPAs based on work substantially less than that done in an audit.

Reviewed financial statements

Financial statements that have been reviewed by independent CPAs who issue their Accountants Review Report.

Safety ratios

These are used to determine a business' exposure to financial risk. Examples of common safety ratios are debt to equity ratio and times interest earned.

Sales and marketing expenses

Costs incurred by a business in promoting and selling its products or services.

Schedules

Work papers prepared to support an entry or account balance.

Seasonality

The effect of a period of the year (season) on a business. For instance, one would presume that an ice cream shop in Alaska makes most of its sales in summer and very few in winter.

Semivariable cost

Costs (such as administrative salaries) that remain static within a relatively small sales volume, then increase or decrease to another static level with a change in sales volume. They may also be referred to as semifixed or step function costs.

Software

The intelligent programs that translate commands and information entered into a computer into signals which can be processed by the computer. See also: Operating system and Application program.

Sole proprietorship

A business that is operated, in unincorporated form, by a single owner.

Source documents

The documents that provide the initial point of entry to an accounting system, such as invoices, checks, and deposit slips.

Spreadsheet

A form of schedule that extends for several columns. Also used to describe several numerical manipulative software programs such as Lotus 1-2-3® (Lotus Corporation) and Excel® (Microsoft Corporation).

Statement of changes in financial position

A financial statement that shows the changes from one balance sheet to another.

Statement of changes in stockholders' equity

A financial statement that shows the reasons why stockholders' equity has changed from one period to the next.

Statement of income

See Income Statement.

Statement of operations

Technically, this is an income statement where the end result is a net loss.

Stock market

The place where securities of "public" companies are traded. The largest stock markets are the New York Stock Exchange (NYSE) and the National Association of Securities/Dealers' Automated Quotation System (NASDAQ). These exchanges provide liquidity for investors by providing a market for their investments and are a source of capital for business.

Stockholders' equity

The amount that the owners have invested in a business. This is represented by paid-in capital plus retained earnings.

Strategy

The broad plan developed by a business.

Supplier

An entity that supplies a business with goods or services.

Tactics

The various short-term ploys developed by a business in implementing its plan or business strategy.

Tangible net worth

A figure considered by banks and some other lenders to be the hard asset value of a business. It is derived by deducting intangibles, such as licenses and patents included as assets on the balance sheet, from net worth.

Times interest earned

A ratio that measures a business' ability to meet interest payments from operating profits. It is calculated as follows:

$$\frac{\text{Earnings before interest and taxes}}{\text{Interest charges}}$$

Total assets

The sum of all assets on the balance sheet.

Total debt to total assets

A ratio that compares total liabilities to total assets and shows how much of the business has been financed by creditors. It is calculated as follows:

$$\frac{\text{Total debt}}{\text{Total assets}}$$

Total liabilities

The sum of all liabilities on the balance sheet.

Total liabilities and stockholders' equity

The sum of all liabilities and stockholders' equity on a balance sheet. This also equals total assets.

Trade terms

The terms under which suppliers agree to supply their customers. The most important tend to be the payment terms, since the supplier is usually extending credit.

Transaction

An economic event that affects the financial affairs of a business. Examples are buying materials and paying wages.

Trend

A general direction, indicating how accounts change over time. For instance, if sales have increased for each of the last three years, there is a trend of increasing sales. However, note that no trend can be observed if less than three time periods are used.

Trial balance

A listing of the balances of all accounts for the same point in time. Historically, this was produced to determine that the general ledger was in balance. It is now normally produced as a useful document from which to prepare financial statements.

Variable cost

A cost that changes in almost exact proportion to volume. An example is the cost of goods sold (cost of sales) tends to change proportionately with sales.

Wholesale

This is where a business sells to other businesses and not to the public. An example is a distributor, who buys from the manufacturer and sells to retail locations, who in turn sell to the public.

Workers' compensation insurance

A required form of insurance for employers, designed to ensure that employees are compensated for work-related accidents.

Working trial balance

A trial balance that is prepared and then amended with subsequent closing entries, arriving at the final trial balance and financial statements.

Index

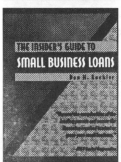

From The Leading Publisher of Small Business Information
Books that save you time and money.

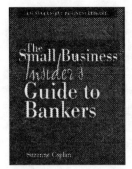

In business, the banker and the institution they represent are often perceived as opponents to your business' success. Shows why business owners should take a leading role in developing and nurturing a worthwhile and lasting partnership with their banker. This inside look will help new, as well as seasoned business owners develop a functional understanding of how the banking industry operates, how to speak their language, and how to turn your banker into an advocate for the growth and success of your small business.

The Small Business Insider's Guide to Bankers   **Pages: 176**
Paperback: $18.95   ISBN: 1-55571-400-5

Clearly reveals the essential ingredients of sound financial management in detail. By monitoring trends in your financial activities, you will be able to uncover potential problems before they become crises. Learn the steps to change your business' cash behavior to get more return for your effort.

Financial Management Techniques   **Pages: 270**
Paperback: $19.95   ISBN: 1-55571-124-3
Binder: $39.95   ISBN: 1-55571-116-2
Software is also available, call for more infomation.

Practical tips on how to turn receivables into cash. Worksheets and checklists help businesses establish credit policies, track accounts, and flag when it's necessary to bring in a collection agency, attorney, or go to court. This book advises how to deal with disputes, negotiate settlements, win in small claims court, and collect on judgments. Gives examples of telephone collection techniques and collection letters.

Collection Techniques for a Small Business   **Pages: 274**
Paperback: $19.95   ISBN: 1-55571-171-5
Binder: $39.95   ISBN: 1-55571-312-2

A comprehensive listing of funding sources. Includes hundreds of current, nationally recognized business loan and venture capital firms. Describes the latest federal, state, county, and community loan, investment, and assistance programs. Gives addresses and phone numbers of federal agency offices in each state.

The Money Connection   **Pages: 274**
Paperback: $24.95   ISBN: 1-55571-351-3
Binder: $39.95   ISBN: 1-55571-352-1

From The Leading Publisher of Small Business Information
Books that save you time and money.

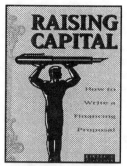

A valuable resource for writing and presenting a winning loan proposal. Includes professional tips on how to write the proposal. Presents detailed examples of the four most common types of proposals to secure venture capital and loans: Private Placement Circular; Prospectus or Public Offering; Financing Proposal; and Limited Partnership Offering.

Raising Capital   **Pages: 160**
Paperback: $19.95   ISBN: **1-55571-305-X**

Straightforward advice on shopping for insurance, understanding types of coverage, and comparing proposals and premium rates. Worksheets help you identify and weigh the risks a particular business is likely to face, then helps determine if any of those might be safely self-insured or eliminated. Request for proposal forms helps businesses avoid over-paying for protection.

The Buyer's Guide to Business Insurance   **Pages: 312**
Paperback: $19.95   ISBN: **1-55571-162-6**
Binder: $39.95   ISBN: **1-55571-310-6**

Demonstrates how the three secrets of customer service (taking care of customers, take care of the organization, and taking care of yourself and your team) make your daily transactions satisfying and productive. Gallagher maintains that the most basic issue behind customer service is the management of the company as a whole and that this directly relates to the concept of fair treatment of all contacts — in-house employees and contractors as well as customers.

Smile Training Isn't Enough   **Pages: 200**
Paperback: $19.95   ISBN: **1-55571-422-6**

An extensive summary of every imaginable tax break that is still available in today's "reform" tax environment. Goes beyond most tax guides on the market that focus on the tax season only, instead it provides you with year-round strategies to lower taxes and avoid common pitfalls. Identifies a wide assortment of tax deduction, fringe benefits, and tax deferrals. Includes a simplified checklist of recent tax law changes with an emphasis on tax breaks.

Top Tax Saving Ideas for Today's Small Business   **Pages: 336**
Paperback: $16.95   ISBN: **1-55571-379-3**

The Oasis Press® Order Form

BOGA08/98

Call, Mail, Email, or Fax Your Order to: PSI Research, P.O. Box 3727, Central Point, OR 97502
Email: sales@psi-research.com   Website: http://www.psi-research.com
Order Phone USA & Canada: +1 800 228-2275   Inquiries & International Orders: +1 541 479-9464 Fax: +1 541 476-1479

TITLE	✔ BINDER	✔ PAPERBACK	QUANTITY	COST
Advertising Without An Agency		❏ $19.95		
Bottom Line Basics	❏ $39.95	❏ $19.95		
BusinessBasics: A Microbusiness Startup Guide		❏ $17.95		
The Business Environmental Handbook	❏ $39.95	❏ $19.95		
Business Owner's Guide to Accounting & Bookkeeping		❏ $19.95		
Buyer's Guide to Business Insurance	❏ $39.95	❏ $19.95		
California Corporation Formation Package	❏ $39.95	❏ $29.95		
Collection Techniques for a Small Business	❏ $39.95	❏ $19.95		
A Company Policy and Personnel Workbook	❏ $49.95	❏ $29.95		
Company Relocation Handbook	❏ $39.95	❏ $19.95		
CompControl: The Secrets of Reducing Worker's Compensation Costs	❏ $39.95	❏ $19.95		
Complete Book of Business Forms		❏ $19.95		
Connecting Online: Creating a Successful Image on the Internet		❏ $21.95		
Customer Engineering: Cutting Edge Selling Strategies	❏ $39.95	❏ $19.95		
Develop & Market Your Creative Ideas		❏ $15.95		
Developing International Markets		❏ $19.95		
Doing Business in Russia		❏ $19.95		
Draw The Line: A Sexual Harassment Free Workplace		❏ $17.95		
Entrepreneurial Decisionmaking		❏ $19.95		
The Essential Corporation Handbook		❏ $21.95		
the Essential Limited Liability Company Handbook	❏ $39.95	❏ $21.95		
Export Now: A Guide for Small Business	❏ $39.95	❏ $24.95		
Financial Decisionmaking: A Guide for the Non-Accountant		❏ $19.95		
Financial Management Techniques for Small Business	❏ $39.95	❏ $19.95		
Financing Your Small Business		❏ $19.95		
Franchise Bible: How to Buy a Franchise or Franchise Your Own Business	❏ $39.95	❏ $24.95		
Friendship Marketing: Growing Your Business by Cultivating Strategic Relationships		❏ $18.95		
Funding High-Tech Ventures		❏ $21.95		
Home Business Made Easy		❏ $19.95		
Information Breakthrough		❏ $22.95		
The Insider's Guide to Small Business Loans	❏ $29.95	❏ $19.95		
InstaCorp – Incorporate In Any State (Book & Software)		❏ $29.95		
Joysticks, Blinking Lights and Thrills		❏ $18.95		
Keeping Score: An Inside Look at Sports Marketing		❏ $18.95		
Know Your Market: How to Do Low-Cost Market Research	❏ $39.95	❏ $19.95		
The Leader's Guide		❏ $19.95		
Legal Expense Defense: How to Control Your Business' Legal Costs and Problems	❏ $39.95	❏ $19.95		
Location, Location, Location: How to Select the Best Site for Your Business		❏ $19.95		
Mail Order Legal Guide	❏ $45.00	❏ $29.95		
Managing People: A Practical Guide		❏ $21.95		
Marketing for the New Millennium: Applying New Techniques		❏ $19.95		
Marketing Mastery: Your Seven Step Guide to Success	❏ $39.95	❏ $19.95		
The Money Connection: Where and How to Apply for Business Loans and Venture Capital	❏ $39.95	❏ $24.95		
Moonlighting: Earn a Second Income at Home		❏ $15.95		
People Investment	❏ $39.95	❏ $19.95		
Power Marketing for Small Business	❏ $39.95	❏ $19.95		
Profit Power: 101 Pointers to Give Your Business a Competitive Edge		❏ $19.95		
Proposal Development: How to Respond and Win the Bid	❏ $39.95	❏ $21.95		
Raising Capital		❏ $19.95		
Renaissance 2000: Liberal Arts Essentials for Tomorrow's Leaders		❏ $22.95		
Retail in Detail: How to Start and Manage a Small Retail Business		❏ $15.95		
Secrets to High Ticket Selling		❏ $19.95		
Secrets to Buying and Selling a Business		❏ $24.95		
Secure Your Future: Financial Planning at Any Age	❏ $39.95	❏ $19.95		
The Small Business Insider's Guide to Bankers		❏ $18.95		
SmartStart Your (State) Business... series		❏ $19.95		
PLEASE SPECIFY WHICH STATE(S) YOU WANT:				
Smile Training Isn't Enough: The Three Secrets to Excellent Customer Service		❏ $19.95		
Start Your Business (Available as a book and disk package)		❏ $ 9.95 (without disk)		

BOOK SUB-TOTAL (Additional titles on other side)

TITLE	✔ BINDER	✔ PAPERBACK	QUANTITY	COST
Starting and Operating a Business in...series *Includes FEDERAL section PLUS ONE STATE section*	❑ $34.95	❑ $27.95		
PLEASE SPECIFY WHICH STATE(S) YOU WANT:				
STATE SECTION ONLY (BINDER NOT INCLUDED) SPECIFY STATE(S):	❑ $8.95			
FEDERAL SECTION ONLY (BINDER NOT INCLUDED)	❑ $12.95			
U.S. EDITION (FEDERAL SECTION – 50 STATES AND WASHINGTON DC IN 11-BINDER SET)	❑ $295.95			
Successful Business Plan: Secrets & Strategies	❑ $49.95	❑ $27.95		
Successful Network Marketing for The 21st Century		❑ $15.95		
Surviving Success		❑ $19.95		
TargetSmart! Database Marketing for the Small Business		❑ $19.95		
Top Tax Saving Ideas for Today's Small Business		❑ $16.95		
Twenty-One Sales in a Sale: What Sales Are You Missing?		❑ $19.95		
Which Business? Help in Selecting Your New Venture		❑ $18.95		
Write Your Own Business Contracts	❑ $39.95	❑ $24.95		
BOOK SUB-TOTAL (Be sure to figure your amount from the previous side)				

OASIS SOFTWARE   Please specify which computer operating system you use (DOS, MacOS, or Windows)

TITLE	✔ Windows	✔ MacOS	Price	QUANTITY	COST
California Corporation Formation Package ASCII Software	❑	❑	$ 39.95		
Company Policy & Personnel Software Text Files	❑	❑	$ 49.95		
Financial Management Techniques (Full Standalone)	❑		$ 99.95		
Financial Templates	❑	❑	$ 69.95		
The Insurance Assistant Software (Full Standalone)	❑		$ 29.95		
Start Your Business (Software for Windows™)	❑		$ 19.95		
Successful Business Plan (Software for Windows™)	❑		$ 99.95		
Successful Business Plan Templates	❑	❑	$ 69.95		
The Survey Genie - Customer Edition (Full Standalone)	❑ $199.95 (WIN)	❑ $149.95 (DOS)			
The Survey Genie - Employee Edition (Full Standalone)	❑ $199.95 (WIN)	❑ $149.95 (DOS)			
SOFTWARE SUB-TOTAL					

BOOK & DISK PACKAGES   Please specify which computer operating system you use (DOS, MacOS, or Windows)

TITLE	✔ Windows	✔ MacOS	✔ Binder	✔ Paperback	QUANTITY	COST
The Buyer's Guide to Business Insurance w/ Insurance Assistant	❑		❑ $ 59.95	❑ $ 39.95		
California Corporation Formation Binder Book & ASCII Software	❑	❑	❑ $ 69.95	❑ $ 59.95		
Company Policy & Personnel Book & Software Text Files	❑	❑	❑ $ 89.95	❑ $ 69.95		
Financial Management Techniques Book & Software	❑		❑ $129.95	❑ $ 119.95		
Start Your Business Paperback & Software (Software for Windows™)	❑			❑ $ 24.95		
Successful Business Plan Book & Software for Windows™	❑		❑ $125.95	❑ $ 109.95		
Successful Business Plan Book & Software Templates	❑	❑	❑ $109.95	❑ $ 89.95		
BOOK & DISK PACKAGE SUB-TOTAL						

AUDIO CASSETTES

TITLE				PAPERBACK	QUANTITY	COST
Power Marketing Tools For Small Business				❑ $ 49.95		
The Secrets To Buying & Selling A Business				❑ $ 49.95		
AUDIO CASSETTES SUB-TOTAL						

Sold To: Please give street address

NAME: _____

Title: _____

Company: _____

Street Address: _____

City/State/Zip: _____

Daytime Phone: _____ Email: _____

Ship To: If different than above, please give alternate street address

NAME: _____

Title: _____

Company: _____

Street Address: _____

City/State/Zip: _____

Daytime Phone: _____

Your Grand Total

SUB-TOTALS (from other side) $ _____

SUB-TOTALS (from this side) $ _____

SHIPPING (see chart below) $ _____

TOTAL ORDER $ _____

If your purchase is:	Shipping costs within the USA:
$0 - $25	$5.00
$25.01 - $50	$6.00
$50.01 - $100	$7.00
$100.01 - $175	$9.00
$175.01 - $250	$13.00
$250.01 - $500	$18.00
$500.01+	4% of total merchandise

07/98

Payment Information: Rush service is available, call for details.
International and Canadian Orders: Please call for quote on shipping.

☐ CHECK Enclosed payable to PSI Research   Charge: ☐ VISA   ☐ MASTERCARD   ☐ AMEX   ☐ DISCOVER

Card Number: _____   Expires: _____

Signature: _____   Name On Card: _____

Use this form to register for an advance notification of updates, new books and software releases, plus special customer discounts!

Please answer these questions to let us know how our products are working for you, and what we could do to serve you better.

Business Owner's Guide to Accounting & Bookkeeping

Rate this product's overall quality of information:
- ☐ Excellent
- ☐ Good
- ☐ Fair
- ☐ Poor

Rate the quality of printed materials:
- ☐ Excellent
- ☐ Good
- ☐ Fair
- ☐ Poor

Rate the format:
- ☐ Excellent
- ☐ Good
- ☐ Fair
- ☐ Poor

Did the product provide what you needed?
- ☐ Yes ☐ No

If not, what should be added?
_____
_____
_____
_____
_____
_____
_____
_____
_____

This product is:
- ☐ Clear and easy to follow
- ☐ Too complicated
- ☐ Too elementary

Were the worksheets easy to use?
- ☐ Yes ☐ No ☐ N/A

Should we include?
- ☐ More worksheets
- ☐ Fewer worksheets
- ☐ No worksheets

How do you feel about the price?
- ☐ Lower than expected
- ☐ About right
- ☐ Too expensive

How many employees are in your company?
- ☐ Under 10 employees
- ☐ 10 - 50 employees
- ☐ 51 - 99 employees
- ☐ 100 - 250 employees
- ☐ Over 250 employees

How many people in the city your company is in?
- ☐ 50,000 - 100,000
- ☐ 100,000 - 500,000
- ☐ 500,000 - 1,000,000
- ☐ Over 1,000,000
- ☐ Rural (Under 50,000)

What is your type of business?
- ☐ Retail
- ☐ Service
- ☐ Government
- ☐ Manufacturing
- ☐ Distributor
- ☐ Education

What types of products or services do you sell?
_____
_____
_____

What is your position in the company?
(please check one)
- ☐ Owner
- ☐ Administrative
- ☐ Sales/Marketing
- ☐ Finance
- ☐ Human Resources
- ☐ Production
- ☐ Operations
- ☐ Computer/MIS

How did you learn about this product?
- ☐ Recommended by a friend
- ☐ Used in a seminar or class
- ☐ Have used other PSI products
- ☐ Received a mailing
- ☐ Saw in bookstore
- ☐ Saw in library
- ☐ Saw review in:
  - ☐ Newspaper
  - ☐ Magazine
  - ☐ Radio/TV

Where did you buy this product?
- ☐ Catalog
- ☐ Bookstore
- ☐ Office supply
- ☐ Consultant

Would you purchase other business tools from us?
- ☐ Yes ☐ No

If so, which products interest you?
- ☐ EXECARDS® Communications Cards
- ☐ Books for business
- ☐ Software

Would you recommend this product to a friend?
- ☐ Yes ☐ No

Do you use a personal computer?
- ☐ Yes ☐ No

If yes, which?
- ☐ Macintosh
- ☐ PC Compatible
- ☐ Other

Check all the ways you use computers?
- ☐ Word processing
- ☐ Accounting
- ☐ Spreadsheet
- ☐ Inventory
- ☐ Order processing
- ☐ Design/Graphics
- ☐ General Data Base
- ☐ Customer Information
- ☐ Scheduling
- ☐ Internet

May we call you to follow up on your comments?
- ☐ Yes ☐ No

May we add your name to our mailing list? ☐ Yes ☐ No

If you'd like us to send associates or friends a catalog, just list names and addresses on back.

Is there anything we should do to improve our products?
_____

Just fill in your name and address here, fold (see back) and mail.

Name _____

Title _____

Company _____

Phone _____

Address _____

City/State/Zip _____

Email Address (Home) _____ (Business) _____

08/98

If you have friends or associates who might appreciate receiving our catalogs, please list here. Thanks!

Name_____ Name_____

Title_____ Title_____

Company_____ Company_____

Phone_____ Phone_____

Address_____ Address_____

Address_____ Address_____

FOLD HERE FIRST

‖‖‖‖

BUSINESS REPLY MAIL

FIRST CLASS MAIL PERMIT NO. 002 MERLIN, OREGON

POSTAGE WILL BE PAID BY ADDRESSEE

PSI Research
PO BOX 1414
Merlin OR 97532-9900

FOLD HERE SECOND, THEN TAPE TOGETHER

✄
Please cut
along this
vertical line,
fold twice,
tape together
and mail.